SCHOOL LIBRARIANSHIP IN THE UNITED KINGDOM

British Library Cataloguing in Publication Data

Pain, Helen
School librarianship in the United Kingdom.
——(British Library information guide,
ISSN 0269-1809; 4)
1. School libraries——Great Britain
I. Title II. British Library. *Research and Development Department* III. Series
027.8'0941 Z675.S3

ISBN 0-7123-3089-5

Helen Pain is a lecturer in the Department of Library and Information Studies at Loughborough University of Technology. She specialises in school and children's public library services, and is course tutor for the MA in School Librarianship. Prior to this her professional career included posts as school librarian and in school library advisory work. As a national committee member of the Library Association's School Library Group, she edits its publications. Her own publications include *Developing a policy for a school library,* and *Implementing a school library policy,* both written jointly with John Lesquereux of Trent Polytechnic, Nottingham, and articles on school library management and the education and training of school librarians. She is also Associate Editor of the *International Review of Children's Literature and Librarianship.*

SCHOOL LIBRARIANSHIP IN THE UNITED KINGDOM

Helen Pain

British Library Information Guide 4

Abstract

The report divides into five main sections: the current state of school libraries in the United Kingdom; the employment of professional librarians in schools; the role of the school librarian; the education and training of school librarians; salaries and conditions of service. There are also 26 appendices, providing more detailed information on all these areas. The information comes from a wide variety of sources, including government and HMI reports, local authority documents and previously unpublished surveys.

British Library Information Guides are published by the British Library Research and Development Department and distributed by the British Library Publications Sales Unit, Boston Spa, Wetherby, West Yorkshire LS23 7BQ, UK. In the USA and Canada they are distributed by Longwood Publishing Group Inc, 27 South Main Street, Wolfeboro, New Hampshire 03894-2069, USA. In Japan they are distributed by Kinokuniya Co Ltd, PO Box 55, Chitose, Tokyo 156, Japan.

ISBN 0 7123 3089 5
ISSN 0269-1809
SI/OPA/282

Typeset by Type Out, London SW16, and printed in Great Britain at the University Press, Cambridge.

Contents

List of tables

1 The current state of school libraries in the United Kingdom

In England and Wales there is no statutory provision for all schools to have libraries, unlike in Scotland and Northern Ireland. In fact most schools do have libraries, but there are tremendous variations in the provision made, their use and their staffing.

This wide variation became clear when the Department of Education and Science published the results of its *Secondary school library survey*[1] in 1981. Replies to a questionnaire were received in 1979 from 386 secondary schools in England; the replies showed that three-quarters of the schools maintained a general library for the whole age range of their pupils, whilst almost all the remaining schools had either sixth form, upper school, or lower school libraries, and frequently a combination of these[2]. The survey showed that in these general libraries:

- the average floor area was 20 sq. m. per 100 pupils;
- there were on average 5.7 study places per 100 pupils;
- access to libraries with an adult in attendance varied as follows:
  4% not available at any time
  83% 10 hours or less
  44% 20 hours or more;
- over 76% were staffed by teachers with no professional librarianship qualifications, compared with 16% staffed by professional librarians. The average number of hours available to teachers staffing school libraries was 19 hours per week. However, there were and still are many examples of teachers having far more limited hours than this;
- the average number of books per pupil was 8.6;
- nearly two-thirds of the stock was non-fiction, and the average additions for 1978/79 were 7% of the library stock;
- the average recurrent expenditure on library books was £93 per 100 pupils for 1978/79, 11% of schools having none.

Tables providing data on staffing, stock and expenditure can be found in Appendix 1.

The Department of Education and Science, through HM Inspectorate

(HMI), has issued more recently two further reports which describe the situation in England. In 1984 the HMI carried out a survey of secondary school libraries in six local education authorities — Isle of Wight, Leeds, Oxfordshire, Sefton, Tameside and Warwickshire[3]. The intention was to assess the adequacy and use of school library provision, and 62 secondary schools, including three sixth form colleges, were visited. The survey revealed a considerable diversity in both provision and use between and within local education authorities. The overall impression was that many libraries were staffed and stocked inadequately, and were poorly financed and under-used[4].

Twelve of the schools, including two of the sixth form colleges, had professional librarians, three of whom were part-time:

> In most of these schools the professional librarian was a considerable asset whose expertise and influence showed itself in greater accessibility, better stock, more effective organisation and, rather less frequently, in greater use by individuals and departments[5].

Forty-nine schools had teacher-librarians, with no professional librarianship qualifications, who had varying amounts of time allocated each week for library duties:

- 19 no time
- 14 1-4 periods per week
- 16 4+ (but usually fewer than 10) periods per week[6].

Ancillary help in the library also varied from 1½ to 37 hours per week in 28 schools, whilst 22 schools had teacher-librarians with both few periods a week allocated to library duties and no ancillary help. In the view of the HMI:

> Some form of adult presence throughout the day is another necessary pre-condition for the development and use of a good library[7].

Low staffing levels and limited time affected detrimentally both the selection, organisation, maintenance and supervision of library stock and the promotion of its use.

It was noted that both professional librarians and teacher-librarians were of low status in the school, and this was reflected in their salary scales. Only 15 attended head of department meetings through having library responsibility, and were therefore involved in the decision-making processes. Access to courses and the qualifications of teachers responsible for school libraries were not encouraging, one teacher being dually qualified in education and librarianship, and eight teachers having the Certificate in School Library Studies which was validated by the Library Association and School Library Association; most of the remainder had attended short day and evening courses organised, for example, by the local authority, school library support services, and the School Libraries Association.

Only three of the libraries surveyed had a multi-media stock, although a desire to develop in this way was expressed by other schools, which stated that inadequate space, finance and staffing were hindering this. Only 20% of the libraries were assessed as having good book provision.

The HMI considered the library as being 'an integral part of the life and work of a school'[8], and yet:

> a major problem was that of the library's inaccessibility to pupils, which was primarily the product of staffing difficulties and the use of the library for other purposes[9].

A desire was expressed by respondents to the survey for advice and guidance in information skills teaching, and in the use of micro-computers for library management, the storing of data, and access to external information sources.

The survey concluded that 'clearly the state of the library and its use in many of these secondary schools gives cause for concern'[10], and the HMI called for there to be a school library policy setting out the place and purpose of the library. By following good practice it was considered that most schools could improve library provision, some substantially so, but in others:

> the investment of money, staff and time is so low that, without a radical change of policy, by the LEA or schools, or in some cases both, no more than minor improvements are likely[11].

The School Libraries Group of the Library Association, in responding to the survey findings, stated that the employment of professional librarians was:

> indicative of a growing trend to capitalise upon the potential that exists in most schools — resources that without the time and expertise of trained librarians would otherwise remain underused and undervalued[12].

The appointment of chartered librarians to all secondary schools is the solution offered by the Group, which urged the government to take the initiative by offering challenge funds to local education authorities for the development of school library resource centres. However, following the report, Bob Dunn, Under-Secretary of State for Education, is reported to have stated that any action to improve the situation must be 'within the constraints of the available resources', and that 'attitudes to school libraries may be at the heart of the issue; and attitudes are not easy to change'[13]. Responding to this the NUT Treasurer Don Winters considered that the attitudes which required changing were those of the Department of Education and Science[14]. Jan Condon, Librarian at Solihull Sixth Form College and editor of *SLG News*, has analysed the survey and produced a checklist of HMI recommendations, and this appears in Appendix 2.

A second HMI report[15], also published in 1985, stated that from the information available to them the Inspectors observed a slight increase of less than 1% of chartered and unchartered librarians in schools, eight authorities showing an increase, 11 a decrease[16]. The report is based upon 1,540 routine visits to maintained schools in England during the autumn term of 1984. From these visits, and the subsequent returns by district Inspectors, the report finds that:

> the provision of libraries in secondary schools was assessed as satisfactory or better in only eighteen LEAs and less than satisfactory or poor in sixty-seven[17].

One of the reasons contributing to this sad picture could be that:

> libraries were said to be often in the hands of hard-pressed teachers who could not attend to more than the routine administration of accession and issue[18].

Also working from the HMI reports, Virginia Berkeley has analysed school library provision and use[19]. She surveyed 26 primary and 26 secondary English schools' full HMI reports, these following week-long visits to each school by 12 to 15 Inspectors. Her findings show that funding is either poor or low; there are deficiencies in both the quality and quantity of stock in most schools surveyed; there are underused libraries; libraries are used as classrooms; generally there is a low level of staffing, only four of the schools, all secondary, having access to chartered librarians. Of these librarians, one served two schools and two were dually qualified as librarians and teachers, and spent a good deal of their time teaching. Where chartered librarians were employed there was evidence of this being appreciated:

> The school is fortunate to have the services of a graduate professional librarian, with all the advantages this brings in terms of organisational and professional advice and expertise[20]. (Kirk Hallam Comprehensive, Ilkeston, Derbyshire.)

However, from these reports it does appear that such appointments are not considered by all Inspectors as essential in providing a library service:

> Although the chartered librarian has been replaced, the library has the benefit of a full-time ancillary assistant . . . the library is well fitted to meeting the developing needs of the college[21]. (Widnes Sixth Form College, Cheshire.)

Such satisfaction is not typical of these reports, however, and recommendations from Inspectors include the need to develop information skills, and also for individual schools to create policies for school libraries, as was recommended in the HMI survey of six authorities described above[22].

The surveys mentioned so far have been concerned solely with England; for an assessment of the provision and adequacy of school libraries in the United Kingdom, one can refer to the survey of expenditure in secondary school libraries produced by the Educational Publishers Council in 1985[23]. In this, 556 schools responded to a questionnaire sent to school librarians in all secondary schools, including independent schools, throughout the United Kingdom.

The average per capita allocation in these schools is shown in Table 1.

Table 1: Average per capita allocation in secondary school libraries[24]

	1981/82	*1982/83*	*1983/84*	*Real term % +/−*
Including independent schools	1.39	1.55	1.59	+2.7
Excluding independent schools	1.31	1.46	1.49	+2.1

Despite there being a slight increase detected between 1981/82 and 1983/84, school librarians complained about cuts to their budgets, or about the static nature of these. Many felt that the school library was seen as a poor relation, and therefore readily subject to cuts in expenditure. They were concerned also that the library was expected to take on board the provision of materials to meet new initiatives in schools, such as computer-assisted learning and the use of video, without extra funding.

The survey shows that the average number of books per head was 10 in maintained schools, and 22 in independent. The mean of capitation allocated to the library was as follows:

1981/82	5.12%
1982/83	5.21%
1983/84	5.05%[25].

Further information on school spending on books can be found in Appendix 3. Half the respondents supplemented their allocations with donations, gifts and sponsored events[26]. Opinion as to the adequacy of the allocation from capitation was generally unfavourable, as Table 2 shows.

Table 2: Adequacy of allocation from capitation[27]

	Including independent schools	*Excluding independent schools*
Inadequate	67.7%	67.5%
Adequate	31.5%	30.0%
Not known	0.8%	2.5%

Concerning staffing of the library, 41% of schools (excluding independents) employed chartered librarians, with or without support, but very often this was on a part-time basis, and 'on occasions, on a salary not appropriate to their qualifications'[28]. The level of staffing was a major cause for concern, and Appendix 4 provides further data on this. Where school libraries were the responsibility of teacher-librarians, comment was made on the inadequate, sometimes non-existent, time allocated for these duties.

The School Libraries Group of the Library Association considered the results of this survey as 'another damning indictment of the lack of will that exists in this country to tackle this problem'[29]. However, one bright note was the incidence of chartered librarians being employed in schools, 41% compared with 16% in the DES *Secondary school library survey* described earlier:

> School libraries without school librarians were recently likened to 'planes without pilots 'stuck on the ground going nowhere'. It appears that trained pilots are being appointed — all that is needed now is the fuel[30].

The Office of Arts and Libraries, as part of the Department of Education and Science, when reviewing the extent of existing central and local government responsibilities for library and information services in 1982, also reported on the state of school libraries[31]. There was uneven development, and attention was drawn to the fact that whilst Education Acts do not refer specifically to the provision of libraries in educational institutions administered by local authorities, they do require them:

> to contribute toward the spiritual, moral, mental and physical development of the community by securing that efficient education... shall be available to meet the needs of the population of the area[32].

Thus, the need to provide libraries in, for example, schools is implicit. School libraries were recognised by the review as part of the national information network, contributing to providing access to information needed by 'individual citizens if they are to play a full and effective role in society'[33]. The Library Association replied to the review, emphasising the urgency of introducing programmes in secondary schools designed to develop information skills, which in turn would require suitably trained staff and supporting library facilities.

The Office of Arts and Libraries, now independent of the Department of Education and Science, has subsequently produced a report[34] which is having a boosting effect on the status of the school library and its role in the school. In his foreword to this report Sir Alan Bullock writes:

> Ten years ago, the Committee under my chairmanship which reported on language, literacy and the schools expressed its concern at the failure to make proper provision for school libraries. This new report... makes clear that the neglect to which we pointed in the 1970s has now become more widespread[35].

He continues, that if materials to support the curriculum:

> are to be provided effectively — and economically — the materials need to be carefully selected, concentrated and co-ordinated, and the [*sic*] calls for the appointment of a librarian whose function needs to be re-defined . . . as 'a teacher whose subject is learning itself'[36].

The report has three main theses: that school libraries and school library services have a vital role to play in educating children to be able to make use of information in formal education and throughout life; that school libraries are underused; that school libraries are under-funded. It warns that:

> the nation will pay a heavy penalty for many years to come if it continues to neglect the self-evident contribution which school libraries could make in producing citizens who are self-reliant, well adjusted and, above all, able to make use of information[37],

and recommends that the educational system should focus upon central curriculum issues, and that these will demonstrate the need for libraries, and lead to 'criteria for resourcing and models for staffing and organisation' being developed with conviction[38]. The staffing should include chartered librarians as these have:

> a unique contribution to make to the educational process and . . . it is desirable that local education authorities should in the longer term continue to seek to employ dually-qualified staff to work as school librarians. In the medium term, until there is a supply of dually-qualified people, we urge an extension of the employment of chartered librarians[39].

The Library and Information Services Councils of both Scotland and Wales endorse the England report. The Welsh Council is in process of undertaking a further report, but with a far wider brief, whilst the Scottish Council has published recently its own report on the present level of library provision for school education in Scotland[40]. Amongst its recommendations this report calls for chartered librarians to be appointed to all secondary schools[41].

The surveys and statements described above demonstrate that all is far from well with school library provision, resourcing and use in the United Kingdom. However, there are three optimistic signs which must not be overlooked. First, the fact that such surveys and statements have been made, all in the last seven years, is indicative of a healthy and developing interest in this area of librarianship. Secondly, that the Department of Education and Science, HM Inspectors, and the Office of Arts and Libraries all demonstrate a concern for the present situation and advocate improvement. Thirdly, that the employment of chartered librarians in secondary schools is heavily recommended, and showing signs of further development.

2 The employment of professional librarians in schools

As stated previously, there are signs of an increase in the employment of professional librarians in secondary schools. Table 3 shows the minimum allocation of staffing, professional, technical and clerical, recommended by the Library Association[42].

Table 3: Allocation of staffing recommended by the Library Association[43]

Number	*Professional staff*	*Clerical*
601-800	1 librarian/ ½ production/ technical asst.	½
801-1000	1 librarian/ 1 production/ technical asst.	1
1001-1500	2 librarians/ 1½ production/ technical assts.	1
over 1500	3 librarians/ 2 production/ technical assts.	2

Schools with separate resource collections in different buildings should provide for a librarian to be available on each site.

It is further recommended that schools with fewer than 600 pupils should be served by peripatetic professional librarians. For many schools these recommendations are highly optimistic.

Where professional librarians are employed, these should preferably be chartered, but salaries, conditions of service and related difficulty in attracting experienced librarians have resulted in some posts being offered to qualified rather than chartered candidates. Not all local authorities employ professional librarians in schools, it being estimated that this is the case in 7% of secondary schools in England and Wales, and 40% in Scotland, which benefited from the implementation of recommendations of the Stimpson Report[44].

The growth of the employment of school librarians can be traced partially from Library Association membership statistics, as shown in Table 4; these can be compared with the number of maintained secondary schools in the United Kingdom, shown in Table 5. However, not all professional librarians working in schools may be members of the Association, and vacancy advertisement statistics give another guide to the employment opportunities which exist. These are presented from an analysis made of the Library Association vacancies supplements in Table 6. The incidence of school librarian employment in Scotland is shown in Appendix 5, and Appendix 6 provides a general view of employment in the counties of England and Wales. Professional librarians are known also to be working in schools in Newcastle upon Tyne, Redbridge borough, Barnet, Sheffield, Bradford, all 11 high schools in Harrow, and the Inner London Education Authority (ILEA), which employs 180. No such posts exist in Northern Ireland schools. Whilst it is possible to gain an estimated view of the number of professional librarians employed in schools throughout the United Kingdom from this information, the exact figure is not known. What can be said, however, is that the number is increasing and affecting schools in many parts of the country.

Whilst knowledge of the existing position is important, equally, if not more so, is that concerning future plans and developments. David Fuegi, Library Adviser in the Office of Arts and Libraries, has been collecting data from local authorities in England and Wales concerning their response to *School libraries: the foundations of the curriculum*[45]. From this data it is seen that many authorities have been using this report to present to their committees strategies for future development, especially in the area of employing chartered librarians in schools. Appendix 7 summarises these data, and presents a most hopeful picture, not least in that 18 authorities state their wish to employ professional librarians in schools.

Table 4: Number of librarians working in schools in the United Kingdom who are also members of the Library Association, 1980-1985

Year	*Total*	*Chartered*	*%*	*Graduate*	*%*	*% of total membership*
1985	710	627	88.31	389	54.79	2.95
1984	690	603	87.39	371	53.77	2.95
1983	712	616	86.52	346	48.60	3.06
1982*						
1981	703	595	84.64	318	45.23	2.92
1980	673	560	83.21	289	42.94	2.98

* No figures available for this year.

Source: Library Association Membership Department.

Table 5: Number of maintained secondary schools in the United Kingdom, 1980-1984

Year	*Total*	*England*	*Wales*	*Scotland*	*Northern Ireland*
1983/84	5327	4444	235	444	204
1982/83	5437	4553	238	442	204
1981/82	5506	4622	241	439	204
1980/81	5542	4654	239	444	205

Source: 1980/83 Central Statistical Office. *Annual abstracts of statistics.* HMSO, 1985, p.89.

1983/84 Department of Education and Science, Welsh Office, Scottish Education Department, Department of Education for Northern Ireland, University Grants Committee. *Education statistics for the United Kingdom 1984 Edition.* HMSO, 1985, p.18.

Table 6: Library Association vacancies supplements — an analysis of vacancies in school librarianship

Area of the United Kingdom	*1981/82*	*1982/83*	*1983/84*	*1984/85*
East	9	8	25	12
London	60(51 ILEA)	19(11 ILEA)	57(51 ILEA)	30(22 ILEA)
Midlands	26	23	40	29
North	14	8	6	8
Overseas	1	–	–	–
South	13	5	4	5
Scotland	22	18	15	27
Wales	2	–	–	–
Totals	147	81	147	111

Breakdown by month and compared with number of vacancies advertised

	1981/82		1982/83		1983/84		1984/85	
	Total	*School posts*	*Total*	*School posts*	*Total*	*School posts*	*Total*	*School posts*
October	61	7	88	10	114	23	131	12
November	60	7	95	9	95	13	122	9
December	49	11	53	2	73	4	79	6+
January	59	8	78	7	113	13	103	8+
February	49	5	88	8	97	8	149	4
March	75	6	not available		135	27	126	8
April	77	13	81	9	102	13	114	4
May	101	28	109	8	119	7	175+	7
June	87	11	123	12	113	17	124	15
July	87	14	99	7	123	9	152	15
August	100	17	93	5	119	6	133	12
September	75	8	102	4	128	7	128	11

Source: Figures collated by Hilary Ghani, Department of Library and Information Studies, Loughborough University. Unpublished.

Whilst Appendix 7 provides data following the impetus of *School libraries: the foundations of the curriculum*[46], other developments, planned before the publication of this report, are found in other local authorities. Harrow, whilst having had a policy of employing chartered librarians in all its high schools and sixth form colleges since 1973, would now like to appoint these to cover groups of primary schools on a peripatetic basis. Derbyshire, employing four full-time and 37 part-time professional librarians in schools, has surveyed its library provision and use in schools and is recommending an increase in full-time posts. Bedfordshire, with 32 chartered librarians in schools, is working towards overcoming the problem of a lack of adequate clerical assistance and funding for training and supply provision. Bradford, with four part-time chartered librarians in schools, has an agreement for similar librarians to be appointed to 20 upper schools, and awaits the agreed 'growth' money on the 1985/86 revenue budget to be released to commence implementation of a rolling programme over five years. Berkshire, with three secondary school professional librarians, has approval for a further three posts but funding has been frozen since 1984/85. Another authority awaiting the availability of finances is Barnet, which has a policy statement made in 1974 recommending the appointment of full-time qualified librarians on a peripatetic basis to cover smaller secondary and primary schools. Hence, finance permitting, extensive developments for improved staffing are ready to come to fulfilment.

The picture in Scotland is similar, with many authorities accepting the principle of professional librarians in schools, but appointing when finance permits. Some authorities have all secondary schools so staffed, for example East Lothian Region, whilst others are almost so staffed, an example being Grampian Regional Council. As stated previously, currently there are no professional librarians working in Northern Ireland schools, despite sizeable school populations and wide-ranging curricula. The employment of, ideally, dual-qualified librarians or chartered librarians in schools is part of a developing long-term policy in Northern Ireland, however, and following the publication of *School libraries: the foundations of the curriculum*[47], a discussion paper has been prepared by the Assistant Chief Librarians (Youth Services) to be presented to the five Education and Library Boards further recommending this.

3 The role of the school librarian

There is no general understanding of a desirable role for the librarian in school, or even of school library practice. Norman Beswick has pointed out that what is considered 'good practice' by Nottinghamshire, Bedfordshire and the ILEA may be quite different from what is so described in the West Midlands, Wales or Norfolk. Equally, what librarians think of as 'good practice' may not agree with the view of teachers, especially if there are resource implications; some approve of libraries, but list them low in their order of priorities. From extensive observations Beswick has noted that on the surface there appears to be little difference between the service offered by teacher-librarians who have been allocated adequate time for their library responsibilities, and that offered by professional librarians. However, with more careful scrutiny the main strength of the professional librarian is seen to be the reference enquiry work undertaken with pupils and teachers, this having more depth and thoroughness. To be effective, however, he recommends that the librarian must be included within the decision-making structure[48].

According to Margaret Meek:

> the role definition depends to a very great extent on the personality of the librarian, her interpretation of her role, the quality of the support given by authorities, especially the head[49].

Later, examples will be provided of how indeed individual librarians have developed their roles, but usually this development arises from a job description for their post, this often having been formulated by the school library service in an advisory capacity to the Education Department. Appendices 8 and 9 provide such descriptions from Nottinghamshire and Newcastle upon Tyne school library services, whilst Appendix 10 contains a description created by an individual school.

To arrive at such job descriptions there has to be a consensus reached as to what role the library, and thereby the librarian, should play in the school. In its guidelines and recommendations for library resource provision in schools the Library Association summarised this role as follows:

> to assist in providing a comprehensive source of learning material

in different formats for use by pupils individually and in small groups; to satisfy curricular, cultural and supplementary requirements, and offer opportunity for loan for use at home; and to provide a store of material and equipment for use by teachers and pupils in classrooms

to organise all relevant learning and teaching material within the school, providing a catalogue which should be readily available in the school library resource centre

to act as liaison within outside agencies and sources of information and encourage their use by pupils and staff

to acquire and disseminate comprehensive information to all staff on materials to meet professional needs and, in co-operation with the school staff, to be actively involved in curricular development within the school as well as maintaining liaison with appropriate outside bodies in this respect

to make its team available for the staff to consult on the selection of appropriate material to achieve their learning objectives

to provide opportunities for staff and pupils to learn how to use the relevant educational material, and training in the exploitation of the facilities of a school library resource centre

to provide facilities, when appropriate, for the production of material within the school by staff and pupils

to provide facilities for the use of audio-visual materials, and to act as agency for the organisation of the maintenance of the relevant technical equipment for the school[50].

In addition, the Association recommends that the school library maintain in its functions the commitment to encouraging reading and 'concern for the enrichment of the individual's imaginative and creative life'[51]. Appendix 11 provides a list of ideas and practices which the 'most successful school libraries' have adopted in order to fulfil these functions, and Appendix 12 comprises a list of the professional roles and tasks which the School Library Association recommends in order for the school library to be effective. These descriptions are extensive and demonstrate that if the roles and tasks are to be fulfilled full-time professional librarians are essential, together with adequate support staff.

In order to identify the purpose of the school library, it is important to 'focus upon central curriculum issues'[52]. School libraries have developed hand in hand with curriculum initiatives, and by continuing to do so can play a vital role in today's schooling. The Department of Education and Science for England and Wales has proposed the following educational aims for schools:

1. to help pupils to develop lively, enquiring minds, the ability to question and argue rationally and to apply themselves to tasks and physical skills

2. to help pupils acquire knowledge and skills relevant to adult life and employment in a fast-changing world

3. to help pupils use language and number effectively

4. to instil respect for religious and moral values, and tolerance of other races, religions and ways of life

5. to help pupils to understand the world in which they live, and the interdependence of individuals, groups and nations

6. to help pupils to appreciate human achievements and aspirations[53].

In all of these aims, which were reiterated in the latest government White Paper on education[54], one can see a role for the school library, and thus the librarian, especially where resource-based learning is taking place within schools. The skills which these aims require developing are shown in Appendix 13, and these appear again in Diagram 1, which shows that in providing materials in a variety of formats the library contributes to relevant learning activities. The government recognises this:

> ... there is much evidence ... that the quality of school work can be improved where LEAs and schools succeed in making available to both primary and secondary pupils an adequate stock of books and other means of information (including new technology) through the school library.... By including library services in its curricular policy, the school is better placed to ensure that the library is fully used to extend the range and depth of learning throughout the school[55].

In addition to information skills development, as the Library Association took pains to point out, the library continues to have its *traditional* role of encouraging and promoting reading, and this too should be part of the curriculum aims:

> In the area of reading, the aims should be to enable pupils to read fluently and with understanding a range of different kinds of material, using reading methods appropriate to the material and the purposes for which they are reading;
>
> to have confidence in their capacities as readers;
>
> to find pleasure in and be voluntary users of reading, for information, for interest, for entertainment, and for the extension of experience and insight that poetry and fiction of quality afford;
>
> to see that reading is necessary for their personal lives, for their learning throughout the curriculum, and for the requirements of living and working in society[56].

Diagram 1: Learning resources and learning activities

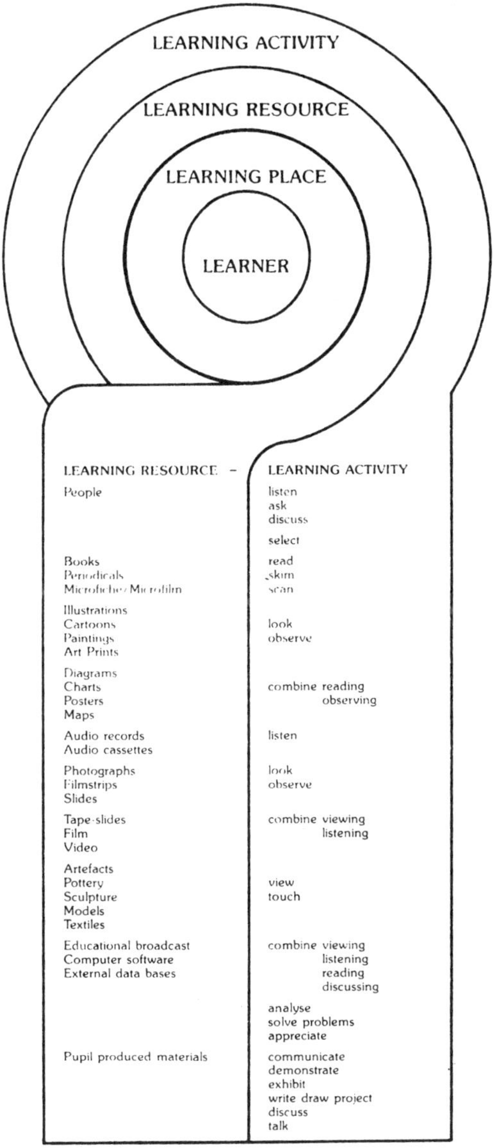

Source: Library and Information Services Committee (Scotland). *Library services and resources for schools education in Scotland. Report of a working party on current provision.* Edinburgh: National Library of Scotland, 1985, p.18. Reproduced by permission.

The implications for school libraries are clear both in the provision of materials and in assisting the development of reading skills, providing opportunities for skills to be practised.

It is not only pupil work undertaken in school which has repercussions on the school library, however. In its recent White Paper on education the government calls for local education authorities and schools to develop homework policies[57]. Subsequently a discussion paper[58] has been produced which includes amongst the reasons for setting homework the encouragement of the development of independent study, the opening up of areas of study, and making possible the use of materials and sources of information not accessible in the classroom[59]. It also suggests that the stock of some school libraries may need to be augmented[60]. The Library Association has responded to this paper[61], defining the role of libraries and librarians regarding homework as providing appropriate materials; giving advice and guidance in selection and use of materials to both teachers and pupils; and making available study facilities for pupils. The major concerns of librarians are seen to be securing sufficient resources of staffing, materials and accommodation; liaison with teachers; and the need to develop library skills teaching and to clarify the complementary roles of teachers and librarians in this work:

> As approaches to learning are changing to a greater emphasis on the pupil as an autonomous learner, the need to teach library and study skills is becoming more widely recognized. Librarians, because of their particular training and experience, have an important role to play in the teaching of library skills and in guiding pupils and teachers to effective use of library resources[62].

The Association recommends the employment of many more professional librarians in schools to support the work of the teachers, especially in the development of information skills:

> . . . because of the cross-curricular nature of the school library, school librarians would be in a good position to support the development of whole school curriculum policies in this area. The appointment of more school librarians and the provision of multi-disciplinary courses in library and study skills teaching need to be developed so that understanding of the particular roles of teachers and librarians can be properly explored and exploited[63].

Homework policies are only one area of development taking place in today's educational system; others include multi-cultural education, the General Certificate of Secondary Education (GCSE), the use of microcomputers, the Technical and Vocational Education Initiative (TVEI) and the Certificate of Pre-Vocational Education (CPVE). Appendix 14 presents a description of the implications of the CPVE on library provision, use, and resourcing, produced by the School Libraries Group of the Library Association as one example of the impact these initiatives can have on school libraries.

The Welsh Office of the Department of Education and Science has presented skills as part of a specification of the curriculum for pupils of 11-16 years of age; these include the ability to use reading skills; to put oneself into other situations, whether of time, place or person; to visualise other experiences; to extract information; to arrange in sequence; to classify; to weigh and interpret evidence and to draw conclusions; to consider other points of view[64]. It is not difficult to see how the school library and librarian can play a useful role in developing these skills:

> There is an educational role for the librarian in the development of learning and problem solving skills, in supporting methods of study, in fostering an attitude of enquiry, of consideration of different viewpoints, and of respect for evidence as a basis for forming judgements and conclusions, in the library and through presentation of its resources[65].

The school library should be seen as integral to the work of the school across the full range of subjects, activities, ages and abilities:

> A well organised and professionally staffed school library optimises the use of resources and contributes to the educational effectiveness of the school. By providing a broad collection of materials, it awakens and expands the pupils' awareness of imaginative literature and of the many varied potential sources of information. The use of resources as an integral part of all subjects taught within the school creates the opportunity for teaching pupils information handling skills which will support them throughout their school careers and prepare them for the future[66].

According to *School libraries: the foundations of the curriculum*[67], librarians as information specialists have been eager to be involved in curriculum developments, even making initiatives in such areas as multi-cultural education and provision, and information skills development:

> We have no doubt that chartered librarians with suitable

> motivation and background have an important contribution to make which goes well beyond the administrative role with which they are sometimes credited . . .[68].

In order to make this contribution, however, school librarians must be included in the school senior management and curricular planning structures; have the opportunity to develop informal links with teaching colleagues; have head of department status and be directly responsible to head-teachers; and be full-time in order to play a full part in the senior management team and offer a comprehensive library service. Further they should have several years of appropriate professional library experience; have appropriate professional maturity to develop the full range of relationships; be chartered librarians; follow suitable programmes of in-service training; and have adequate support staff[69].

When examining successful curriculum initiatives certain key elements which have led to this success can be identified, these being professionally up-to-date teaching staff; an ever widening range of resources; concentration on a variety of intellectual and practical skills; a centre where independent work (by both staff and pupils) can be developed; extensive stocks of materials; and an awareness on the part of the whole school of the curriculum development taking place[70]. Such key elements demonstrate the need for the provision of well-resourced school libraries staffed by chartered librarians, with adequate support staff, to stock, organise, and promote the service and use of materials for work, information and pleasure; librarians who are actively involved in a pro-active role in curriculum planning and development, and who are important sources of professional support and information to all teaching staff:

> The employment of chartered librarians by Nottinghamshire has ensured that a high degree of professionalism is brought to bear, whether marginal, bibliographic or curricular issues are concerned. The growing emphasis on skills as well as knowledge content within the curriculum means that the librarian will continue to have a stimulating and demanding contribution to make within the school to the benefit of both librarianship and education[71].

What has been achieved : some examples

Professional librarians working in schools have contributed greatly to the increased awareness of their value. Good practice has been implemented, observed and followed to the benefit of pupils and teacher alike. Appendix 15 provides a list of library aims and objectives compiled by such a librarian, who has considered the school served and the needs of both pupils and teachers in deciding the library's role within the school. But what does such a list look like when interpreted into day-to-day activity? Appendices 16 and 17 provide some evidence of the varied and demanding nature of the work involved, and demonstrate the extensive expertise required of the school librarian. The diary, in particular, shows the fragmented nature of the day, and that whilst the librarian's timetable represents that of a teacher there are no free periods, the librarian being on duty even during break and lunch times.

The job description for the librarian at the Margaret Dane School (Appendix 10) shows that she has a central position in the school's planning and implementation of resource-based learning, being seen 'at the forefront of innovations in the curriculum'[72]. She attends staff meetings, departmental meetings, co-ordinating committee meetings in connection with study skills, and meetings of the primary-secondary liaison committee, participating and innovating:

> . . . the librarian made space for the extension of professional co-operation, the breaking down of traditional subject barriers and the possibility of new work of all kinds[73].

It is vital that the school librarian works in close collaboration with the teachers, forming a team working towards the educational aims of the school to the benefit of the pupils. In order to be able to support the work of the school the librarian must be aware of the different learning needs of the children with varied learning abilities; have a knowledge of the range of skills pupils require to learn, of the teachers' objectives and the desired learning outcomes; recognise the needs of pupils to acquire progressively competence in increasingly complex information skills; and as pupils move to student-centred learning develop an understanding of the purpose of problem-solving, assignments, projects, independent study and resource-based learning[74]. This implies that the school librarian must work in close consultation with the teachers. The librarian at Wandsworth School, London, attends all committee meetings of the heads of department, resources group, book-shop group, computer group, and the curriculum review body, and co-operates with the multi-cultural committee[75]. The librarian at the Park Comprehensive, Nottingham, attends all curricular meetings to maintain an awareness and for liaison, in order to ensure that stock is relevant and services are provided to support curricular needs[76].

The HMI report on school libraries in six local education authorities found that concerning the teaching of information skills there was a 'great deal of interest, but comparatively little actual practice'[77]. However, this observation does not apply to all schools, especially not those which employ professional librarians. For example, at Heaton Manor School, Newcastle upon Tyne, there is a good deal of activity as described by the Newcastle School Library Service. During one academic year the librarian at Heaton Manor School deals with a 12 form entry, providing one library lesson per week for the first two terms of the school year.

In addition the study skills module of the sixth form guidance programme and the Humanities Department language skills programme occupy a further six periods each week.

The librarian at the Margaret Dane School has inaugurated a programme for extending skills, each department having been asked to specify which skills should be concentrated upon. This resulted in a list of competencies to be fostered, and induction courses were prepared for third, fourth and sixth form pupils. The movement is towards the integration of these skills into the curriculum, with reinforcement in subject classes[78].

At Stonelaw High School, Glasgow, first and second year pupils experience a specially structured programme of user education, whilst pupils taking the Certificate of Sixth Year Studies in English are taught in the library, as part of their coursework requires them to produce a literary dissertation, the planning discussions of which involve the librarian, listening to ideas and suggesting methods for retrieving background information. There is further involvement in first year projects set by the Modern Studies Department to promote project skills, and a step-by-step guide has been prepared showing how to choose a topic; on the information required; on sources of information in and outside the library; on the use of information and the importance of relevance and originality. To support this type of work the library maintains a 'Hot Line Box', an alphabetical listing of popular project topics giving names, addresses, and telephone numbers of organisations, clubs, societies and individuals who welcome enquiries. It also has 'Fact Files' of information in pictures, newspaper cuttings, handouts and booklets on subjects of current interest, such as vivisection and solvent abuse. In addition, the librarian of this school provides skill lessons tailored to the needs of subject departments[79].

The librarian at Wandsworth School, London, also has a structured information skills course, which starts from the point of view that reading is pleasure. This course commences with first year pupils and is reinforced in the second year[80].

At Park Comprehensive, Nottingham, there is an emphasis upon the development of study skills and resource-based learning. The librarian is a member of the first year Integrated Study Team, and the library skills of information retrieval and evaluation, together with study skills, are an integral part of the first year course. These skills are reinforced through school:

> The recognition of the increasing need for pupils to develop these information skills, for study and later adult life, has led to the librarian's skills playing an important role in the support of this part of the curriculum[81].

All the first year pupils at Park Comprehensive attend a formal induction course of five sessions which cover locational, retrieval, reference and informational skills through a structured course and game simulations. These skills, including library skills, are then reinforced through resource-based learning, and are tested during end-of-year examinations. Following these, pupils identified as needing further help are taught in small groups. Reinforcement of skills continues throughout the school, for example in library-based research-orientated work, an indication of the variety of which can be gained from Appendix 18.

One area of skill development which has come fairly recently to the fore in some school libraries is that related to the use of microcomputers as sources of information. A survey by the BBC and the Microelectronics Education Programme (MEP) found that 98% of secondary schools possessed a microcomputer, the average number of microcomputers for all schools so equipped being 8.7[82]. However, the Department of Education and Science survey of six local education authorities found only three school libraries with micros, and these being used for a limited range of organisational tasks, although a potential was recognised for their use in management, data storage and access to external information sources[83]. One can add to this list the development of information skills, in order that the adults of the future, who will be expected to use computers in satisfying their information needs as they do books and other printed materials to-day, are equipped to use these sources effectively and efficiently:

> The advent of microcomputers, providing information storage, manipulation and retrieval capacity relatively cheaply and conveniently throughout the school, makes it essential for the role of

> the library/resource centre in information technology to be considered and developed systematically[84].

A number of Nottinghamshire school librarians are working together creating information files:

> The school library/resource centre is generally regarded as a 'neutral', cross-curricular, whole-school facility, which is accessible to pupils, and often open longer hours than other parts of the school, and it is therefore an obvious place to house at least one of the school's microcomputers, perhaps with Prestel and Ceefax/Oracle links, thus providing staff and pupils with access to a whole new range of information sources including school created databases and co-operatively produced information files.
>
> Pupils would benefit from seeing and operating a working system, and the development of study skills courses, including information technology, would further enhance the immediacy and relevance of such provision[85].

The librarian at Holgate Comprehensive, Hucknall, has been active particularly in using micros as part of his information skills programme, and has created his own programs for this purpose, some of which he has made available commercially.

Bedfordshire is another authority in which the school librarians have worked co-operatively in developing expertise in the use of information retrieval packages, evaluating programs, and developing databases. Appendix 19 lists some of the databases which have been created so far.

At Wandsworth School, London, a microcomputer is available in the library for pupils to use. There is a small collection of programs, including word-processing packages, Schools Information Retrieval (SIR) and many SMILE mathematics games. The aim is to generate computer familiarity, providing pupils with the opportunity to experiment and practise away from the classroom. Pupils have created their own programs, and staff use the word-processor, or try out computer-assisted learning packages. The development of skills employed in database use is seen as a natural development from book-based information skills[86].

In 1979 the Department of Education and Science published the findings of a survey of English secondary education in which it was stated that:

the school library is the most important single contribution of all the school's reading resources[87].

The library and librarian at Stonelaw High School certainly support this statement. There the English department requires all first and second year pupils to read at least three books from the library's fiction booklist, and to write short reviews. To encourage those readers who prefer non-fiction the librarian has devised displays of fiction categories, such as adventure and science fiction. Each display is maintained for one month, with titles being changed regularly. These have proved so popular with the whole school that senior fiction for pupils and staff is now included. Further reading promotion takes the form of storytelling, quizzes, drama improvisation and mime, as regular events[88].

The librarian at Wandsworth School, London, has since 1981 organised visits to the school from authors twice a term. In the same year as the inception of this enterprise, a book fair was held during one afternoon involving 30 authors, artists and storytellers, and a working exhibition on book-making, puppets, clowns and sideshows. Children from local primary schools and a school for partially sighted children were invited to attend with the school's own pupils. In total 900 children attended and a subsequent increase in the demand for books was noted. The librarian has worked closely with the English, Art and History departments in putting on an exhibition of second year work created in response to reading Robert Westall's *The machine gunners.* This resulted in models, paintings, poems, essays, stories, souvenirs of World War II loaned by grandparents, and drama props being put on show in the library. This school's librarian also provides a bookshop, thus encouraging book ownership[89].

The librarian at Park Comprehensive, Nottingham, also runs a bookshop and organises bookfairs. New literature is introduced by relating fiction to teaching themes, and magazines are considered important in encouraging reading, especially by reluctant readers. The library plays a key part in departmental teaching, in providing teaching material and in extra-curricular activities. The atmosphere is welcoming, and the stock is visually exciting, well displayed and selected to appeal to all abilities[90].

The school library should be a source of information, both professional and local. Stonelaw High School, Glasgow, provides information on local and school events for junior and senior noticeboards[91], and the librarian at the Margaret Dane School instituted a community information project 'What's on locally?'[92]. Library activities are listed in Wandsworth School's weekly bulletin, and the librarian there provides an appreciated professional information service for teachers, photocopying relevant articles, and making and circulating selective lists of additions to stock or materials of particular interest:

> The library is the first place I turn to with their excellent section of education[93].

An area of particular current interest and concern is the development of libraries which encourage multi-cultural awareness. In Margaret Marshall MacDonald's case study of Wandsworth School, London, a section is allocated to the librarian, describing her role as follows:

> 5. To provide a comprehensive and relevant multi-cultural resource centre.
>
> World religions, culture, legends, literature and history are represented in as accessible a form as can be found. There are some books in non-European languages, mainly to give their speakers a sense of familiarity. Too many community languages are represented in school for it to be possible to form a worthwhile collection as a permanent holding, but there are several sources to borrow from including the local Public Library Service. The posters to be seen on the walls of the library reflect the multi-cultural nature of our society and the different languages spoken. I choose materials which offer positive views rather than stereotypes, particularly in areas of gender, race and culture. Current writing which offends against such principles is not likely to be purchased. Books from earlier periods, however, come into a different category. Even if considered lacking when judged by present standards of awareness, such books may be of historical interest or have other values, and I prefer to keep them, and discuss their point of view or bias with their users. We hold exhibitions of resources including films and music and these familiarise staff and boys with the extent of the stock. The number of items borrowed on these occasions indicates how useful they are found to be[94].

Gillian Klein has commented also on the dynamic role of the library in developing multi-cultural education, and describes an inner city comprehensive, identity not made known, where the concern of the librarian:

> with regard to the treatment of racial issues in all the materials purchased, used and produced in the school has pervaded the

curriculum materials and highlighted the sensitivities of the staff as a whole.

The LRC also supports multicultural developments in curriculum and in theoretical considerations by seeking out and promoting appropriate materials and by putting relevant reading matter on multicultural education into the hands of the staff[95].

4 The education and training of school librarians

> It is not usually recognized that school librarians usually begin their professional careers outside school and without special reference to children. Those who develop particular interests in school libraries do so because they have a concern about the evolution of librarianship firstly in relation to the changing needs of learners, and secondly because the school library offers a particular kind of challenge in matching its stock to the width of its use as designed by the variety of the needs of its users, and their growing accomplishments in finding their way to learning[96].

As shown above, the role of the school librarian is challenging, varied and arduous, though at the same time it can be satisfying and rewarding. What are the competencies expected of such a professional?

> It is a task that requires a mature and experienced librarian, capable of working under pressure for long periods, of working in professional isolation and requiring a breadth of knowledge that will enable them to integrate fully into the school and to understand the demands of teaching and we have been fortunate in Bedfordshire in attracting many staff of a very high calibre into the school library service[97].

After 33 years of experience in and around librarianship and education, Norman Beswick is convinced that there is no job in librarianship which demands a wider spread of professional librarianship understanding, and which requires — and seems to bring out — a wider range of personal qualities. The ability to succeed in school librarianship is dependent not only on qualifications, but also on knowledge, self-confidence and perceptiveness, which qualifications and other experiences and learning have created[98].

Appendix 20 provides a list of areas of knowledge and understanding considered to be essential to the good school librarian's work. Norman Beswick considers the librarian is well prepared in the areas of selection of materials, reference and enquiry work, the organisation of knowledge and the organisation and management of the library, and even the area concerned with the personal development of the child, depending on the courses he or she has followed. However, there is a problem with the first area of knowledge, that concerning curriculum studies, learning theory and teaching methodologies. This knowledge may be picked up from experience, but knowledge so gained does not guarantee that the school librarian can talk with authority on these subjects. This can thus be seen as the key element lacking in the librarian's qualifications, and Norman Beswick suggests that school librarians require the in-depth skills of a chartered librarian and some understanding of education[99].

This view would appear to be borne out by a survey of competencies required by school librarians, undertaken in 1984. Readers of the *SLG News* who were also practising professional school librarians were asked to identify the competencies which they considered school librarians required. Previously, professional school librarians in Nottinghamshire had been asked to list the knowledge, skills and attitudes required by school librarians, and their response provided a check list for *SLG News* readers to identify essential, desirable and unnecessary competencies. The intention behind this exercise was to inform those concerned with the education of school librarians, particularly at Loughborough University.

In total 43 responses were received, and the results are shown in Appendix 21. It was not surprising to find that few respondents considered any of the competencies not required, as the original list was composed by practising school librarians. However, additional competencies were suggested: to knowledge was added art and crafts, educational management and support services; to skills, art and crafts, innovatory skills, typewriting and salesmanship; to attitudes, non-sexist attitudes, non-racist attitudes and willingness to listen[100].

The results of the survey no doubt reflect the role of the school librarians within their schools, and from this viewpoint prove most interesting. For example, one can make a general assessment of the impact of computers by noting that the majority of respondents considered the operation of a computer a desirable rather than an essential skill. The weight of emphasis upon technical and reprographic knowledge and skills probably further demonstrates the school librarian's involvement. One surprise was that of all the attitudes only one — sagacity — was considered to be desirable rather than essential, and for this reason it is not included in the list in Appendix 21.

This sample is small, given the number of professional librarians working in school libraries; however, the results are similar to impressions gained from conversations with those concerned with this area of librarianship and from reading reports of related research such as that undertaken by Pfister[101]. For educators of prospective school librarians the *SLG News* survey presents a good deal of food for thought, including the following:

— *general knowledge and a good academic educational background*

* Can achieving a place in higher education indicate both?

* Where interviews are short, or non-existent, can references, academic record, interests and hobbies be relied upon as adequate and accurate assessments of candidates?

* Interviews should incorporate general questions relating to current affairs, awareness of and participation in local events and initiatives, as well as concerning career choice.

* Should General Studies be recognised by those institutions which do not include this in their A level requirements?

* Study in higher education of an additional, and some might say more academically recognisable, subject, as well as librarianship, assists towards the desired academic education background.

* O and A level grades and class of degree provide some guidance as to academic ability, but how far do they describe the overall person or reflect total education?

— *child/teenage development and behaviour*

* This is an important part of education studies, where theoretical studies of child psychology and teacher-pupil relationships are supported by teaching practice which provides eye-to-eye contact with pupils regularly for at least 16 weeks, and students may be asked to write an in-depth child study. Education options such as adolescence, or children with special learning needs, add to this experience and knowledge which in turn develop confidence and authority.

* Librarianship courses sometimes include core, optional or a combination of courses which relate to school librarianship as an aspect of children's library work. These should, and usually do, include background on child and teenage development, but usually not the in-depth study or contact described above.

— *librarianship*

* All school librarians require a sound, basic library education background.

* There should also be the opportunity for prospective school librarians to study specialised subjects such as the role of the library in education supporting teaching and learning; the production of materials; publishing and the book trade; marketing; public speaking; display work; selection and assessment of adult and children's materials, including software. There should also be opportunities for general theories — for example, information searching and indexing — to be related to circumstances in schools.

— *education*

* The knowledge and skills cited in the survey are those found in the education and training of teachers. Library studies option courses can provide an insight, but not in-depth study.

— *management*

* This should be a compulsory part of every librarian's education, as all become managers, some even in their first post. Even school librarians, often lacking in support staff, are part of the management structure of the school and need the skills and knowledge of management, as the survey shows.

* General management theory should be related to specialised fields of librarianship, such as school librarianship.

— *new technology*

* This should be integrated into the library school curriculum.

* School librarians should be cognisant of the relevance of both computers and audio-visual technology to education as well as librarianship.

* They should be aware of the application of computers, to library administration, information handling and searching, compilation of databases, and the design of computerised information skills programmes.

* They should be able to assist pupils using computers, which are found increasingly in school libraries, and be able to locate and select computer software which, with audio-visual aids, should be seen as an integral part of library stock.

* They should have a detailed knowledge of the learning and teaching potential of different media. Increasingly schools are producing their own materials, and basic knowledge of the principles of reprographics, layout design and readability is necessary.

— *attitudes*

* Some of those listed may be present in the prospective student, but identification is difficult at interview, especially if the candidate is a school leaver yet to mature.

* The educational process can encourage the development of some of the desired attitudes, especially through using learning methods which encourage discussion, problem-solving, student initiative, working in groups and individually, and developing a pride in one's profession, understanding its important contribution to the lives of others.

For some years now there has been lively debate as to the desirability of school librarians being dually qualified as professional librarians and teachers. The Library Association recommends as follows:

> We believe that all experience points to the overriding importance to the school librarian of the understanding and confidence given by full professional qualifications and suitable work experience in librarianship. We are convinced that the education and training of a professional librarian ensures that he or she is fully equipped to undertake the duties required in a school library resource centre. At the same time, knowledge and understanding of the theory and practice of education is desirable.
>
> On this matter, the Bullock Report, *A language for life*, recommends that 'as a long term aim all school librarians should be doubly qualified in teaching and librarianship'. (Rec.277.) Although opportunities for obtaining double qualifications are improving, it will be many years before there is a sufficient number of such people available to schools. Nevertheless this trend towards dual qualification will continue and must be taken account of[102].

The School Library Association also officially endorses dual qualification as the ideal. However, dual qualification is difficult to attain, and the financial and career incentives are recognised as insufficient in *School libraries: the foundations of the curriculum*, which, however, recommends that in the longer term dually qualified staff should be employed as school librarians[103]. Whilst recognising the need for knowledge of educational practice and curriculum developments in the professional training of school librarians, a seminar in Scotland in 1984 recommended that practising school librarians should be able to obtain this additional knowledge, or some qualification in these subject areas[104]. This recommendation is in step with a good deal of present-day thinking on this issue, which suggests that rather than providing first professional courses aimed at producing school librarians there should be instead a continuing education programme open to those chartered librarians either wishing to enter this field of librarianship, or who are practising school librarians. However, the creating of an awareness of school libraries as being part of the library and information service network, together with their particular characteristics, should be included in first professional courses, be they undergraduate or postgraduate.

The School Libraries Group of the Library Association has made a pronouncement on the subject of educating school librarians which makes the following points:

— Professional education of school librarians 'should commence with a formal academic course covering all aspects related to the information environment'.

— All students should become aware of school libraries and their support services.

— When electives are offered, these should include school librarianship.

— There is a concern that some library schools, particularly those with a high proportion of postgraduate students, omit school librarianship from their curriculum. Other library schools which had such options have curtailed elements of school library education recently, or ceased offering these altogether, and yet school librarianship is of increasing importance in terms of manpower requirements.

— There is a need to recognise the educational nature of library work in schools.

— There is a need also to develop post-initial qualifications and continuing education courses in school librarianship, possibly offered by fewer library schools 'which by their specialization are considered centres of excellence in school librarianship'.

— The post of school librarian is not suitable for the newly qualified, and there is a 'need for continuing education, both to update expertise and to enable librarians whose early specializations have been in other fields, to equip themselves as school librarians'.

— Reports and documents are stressing the need for dual qualification, and the problem of obtaining these qualifications must be addressed. Realistic opportunities must be provided for teachers and librarians to obtain these qualifications. Distance learning and short in-college attendance, with course credits being earned, must be considered.

— Recommended competencies include a knowledge of educational development; communication and information skills; the development of information services; management of resources; policy development; and computers[105].

These thoughts are very much shared by others concerned with this matter. In discussion following papers presented at a one-day workshop, 'Educating school librarians', two points were made in favour of continuing education. Firstly, that further qualifications enhance status. Secondly, that the study of education provides a school librarian with the opportunity to see the library through the eyes of a teacher, developing an awareness of teachers' ideas and points of view, leading to potentially fruitful teamwork[106]. At this same workshop, Norman Beswick described how other countries with developed school libraries expected school librarians first to qualify as teachers, and then to acquire an additional librarianship qualification. It is assumed also that the school librarian's work experience will be wholly in schools. The flexible higher education systems of some countries permit the gradual acquisition of a range of qualifications and higher degrees through part-time and summer study. The problems in the United Kingdom prohibiting a similar development are, in his opinion, the higher education system, the grant and secondment position, and the lack of recognition of additional qualifications by way of improved salaries and conditions of service[107].

School libraries: the foundations of the curriculum urges consideration of the:

> establishment of new training programmes on a modular basis, targeted at the eventual attainment of a qualification meaningful in academic terms, career terms, and in terms of professional acceptance[108].

The Scottish partner of this report suggested that it would be helpful to investigate ways in which joint courses could be offered between departments of Librarianship and Education, once again recommending part-time modular courses with a system of credits, involving distance learning, seminars and assessment of practical work, for librarians in post[109]. Appendix 22 lists the elements which this report recommends for inclusion in advanced courses of study for school librarians.

Part-time, modular courses have been recommended also by Sheila Ray, who notes the Department of Education and Science's recommendation for employers to value part-time study and support this with study time and fees[110]. She also voices concern over the availability in library schools of courses concerned with school librarianship and related areas, and this too is shared by many in the profession, as already noticed in the School Libraries Group's pronouncement [111]. Appendix 23 contains the results of a survey of United Kingdom library schools, which demonstrates what is taught, in what context, for how long and to whom.

5 The salaries and conditions of service of school librarians

There is a good deal of discontent concerning the salaries and conditions of service of school librarians. The present promotion and salary structure is seen not to 'reflect their aspirations of current curricular developments and librarians' practical contributions to these'[112].

School libraries: the foundations of the curriculum stated that evidence the working party had received demonstrated low pay and low status, together with the lack of a self-evident career structure[113].

The salaries and conditions of service for most school librarians are according to the National Joint Council for Local Authorities' Scheme of Conditions of Service for England and Wales, and the National Joint Council for Local Authorities' Services (Scottish Council) for Scotland. It is recommended that they should be paid on a scale of no fewer than six incremental points, by linking consecutive National Joint Council grades as necessary, in order for career commitment and development to be possible. Further, it is recommended that in order to attract and retain school librarians of an appropriate calibre, they must be paid on scales above those paid to librarians undertaking basic duties under supervision. The basic grade for a school librarian should be spiral column points 31-36, SO1/SO2, this basic grade being extended to take into account size of school, the number of sites, the breadth of the school's curriculum and resourcing needs, and whether located in an Education Priority Area[114]. Appendix 24 provides a guide to scales and equivalent salaries. Unfortunately these recommendations are rarely met by local authorities, librarians, in common with other 'non-teaching' staffs in schools and colleges, being 'poorly paid . . . and subject to conditions of service that would not be tolerated for other APT and C staff'[115].

Whilst the survey of vacancies in the Library Association vacancies supplements from 1981-1985 showed that there has been improvement in minimum salaries, i.e.:

1981/82	67% posts with minimum salary £5,500
1982/83	75% posts with minimum salary £5,500
1983/84	66% posts with minimum salary £5,600
1984/85	56% posts with minimum salary £6,300[116],

there is a long way to go before recommendations will be met.

Appendix 25 provides examples of salaries offered by authorities, demonstrating variety, and the unique salaries of the ILEA. The Association of Librarians in Schools (Nottinghamshire) has produced a comparison of librarians' salaries with those of teachers and school secretaries, and whilst this relates to 1983/84 it still makes interesting reading. Even with the improvement of Nottinghamshire salaries there is still no parity between salary and head of department status (Appendix 26).

Both Nalgo[117] and the Library Association[118] recommend that there should be greater flexibility as to when school librarians can take leave; at present this is usually restricted to school holidays. The Library Association also recommends that as school librarians work extra hours during term times — during lunch breaks, or attending meetings after school — compensation for these in the form of annual leave or other appropriate arrangements should be considered[119]. A further recommendation is that opportunities to undertake training and professional development should be no less favourable than those of their professional and teaching colleagues[120].

Without doubt there is a need for the ratification and improvement of salaries and conditions of employment if school librarians are to achieve their desired role. A career structure must be created:

> Where additional posts for professional librarians are provided in schools, these could be open to pre-Licentiates and Licentiates as training ground for school librarianship[121].

Also, promotional opportunities for school librarians must be developed in order to maximise their experience to the benefit of education, rather than having them leave school librarianship for personal and financial advancement.

Salaries must be seen to reflect the responsibilities, qualifications and experience of school librarians, equating to head of department, their recommended status. However, salaries are not the only area of parity required to improve the status of the librarian in the school; attention also needs to be paid to leave, training, and staffing relief for attending courses, maternity leave and sickness.

One of the major problems to-day is attracting and keeping the right kind of librarian in school librarianship. It is salary and conditions of service which hold the key for future development in meeting the employment demands, providing additional education and training, and ensuring the acceptance of the school librarian in the school as a fellow professional:

> The school librarian has an important function in the life of the school, and we would wish it to be recognised with appropriate salary, career prospects and status[122].

6 References

1. Great Britain, Department of Education and Science. *Secondary school library survey.* HMSO, 1981. (Statistical Bulletin 7/81.)

2. Ibid., p.1.

3. Great Britain, Department of Education and Science. *Report by HM Inspectors on a survey of secondary school libraries in six local education authorities. Carried out February-May 1984.* Department of Education and Science, 1985.

4. Ibid., p.2.

5. Ibid., p.4.

6. Ibid.

7. Ibid., p.5.

8. Ibid., p.15.

9. Ibid., p.14.

10. Ibid., p.20.

11. Ibid., p.21.

12. School Libraries Group, Library Association. Press release.

13. Dunn, B, quoted in *The Teacher* 41(41), 28 June 1985.

14. Winters, D, quoted in *The Teacher* 41(41), 28 June 1985.

15. Great Britain, Department of Education and Science. *Report of HM's Inspectors on the effects of local authority expenditure policies on education provision in England — 1984.* Department of Education and Science, 1985.

16. Ibid., p.24.

17. Ibid.

18. Ibid.

19. Berkeley, V. School library provision and use: a review of HMI reports. *Journal of Librarianship* 17(2), April 1985, pp.106-118.

20. Ibid., p.112.

21. Ibid.

22. Great Britain, Department of Education and Science. *Report by HM Inspectors on a survey of secondary school libraries in six local education authorities. Carried out February-May 1984.* Department of Education and Science, 1985.

23. *Survey on expenditure in secondary school libraries.* Educational Publishers Council, 1985.

24. Ibid., p.2.

25. Ibid., p.5.

26. Ibid., p.12.

27. Ibid., p.14.

28. Ibid., p.4.

29. Library books cash cut. *The Teacher* 41(43), 12 July 1985.

30. Ibid.

31. Great Britain, Department of Education and Science, Office of Arts and Libraries. *The future development of libraries and information services.* HMSO, 1982.

32. Ibid., p.7.

33. Ibid.

34. Great Britain, Office of Arts and Libraries. *School libraries : the foundations of the curriculum. Report of the Library and Information Services Council's Working Party on school library services.* HMSO, 1984. (Library Information Series No.13.)

35. Ibid., p.iv.

36. Ibid., p.v.

37. Ibid., p.1.

38. Ibid., p.7.

39. Ibid., p.12.

40. Library and Information Services Committee (Scotland). *Library services and resources for school education in Scotland. Report of a working party on current provision.* Edinburgh: National Library of Scotland, 1985.

41. Ibid., p.47.

42. *Library resource provision in schools: guidelines and recommendations.* Library Association, 1977, p.16.

43. Ibid.

44. *Non-teaching staff in secondary schools. Report of a working party appointed by the Secretary of State for Scotland.* HMSO, 1976.

45. Great Britain, Office of Arts and Libraries. *School libraries: the foundations of the curriculum. Report of the Library and Information Services Council's Working Party on school library services.* HMSO, 1984. (Library Information Series No.13.)

46. Ibid.

47. Ibid.

48. Beswick NW. Knowledge and skill requirements of the school librarian. Lecture given at a one-day workshop on *Educating school librarians*, organised by the School Libraries Group, and held at Loughborough University on 25 September 1985.

49. Thomson, L and Meek, M. *Developing resource-based learning: one school's approach.* Longman, 1985, p.84.

50. *Library resource provision in schools: guidelines and recommendations.* Library Association, 1977, pp.10-11.

51. Ibid., p.11.

52. Great Britain, Office of Arts and Libraries. *School libraries: the*

foundations of the curriculum. Report of the Library and Information Services Council's Working Party on school library services. HMSO, 1984. (Library Information Series No.13.)

53. Great Britain, Department of Education and Science, Her Majesty's Inspectorate. *The school curriculum.* HMSO, 1981.

54. Great Britain, Department of Education and Science. *Better schools.* HMSO, March 1985. (Cmnd 9469.)

55. Ibid., p.26.

56. Great Britain, Department of Education and Science. *English from 5-16.* HMSO, 1984, p.2. (Curriculum Matters 1.)

57. Great Britain, Department of Education and Science. *Better schools.* HMSO, March 1985, p.25. (Cmnd 9469.)

58. Great Britain, Department of Education and Science. *Homework discussion paper.* Department of Education and Science. April 1985. (DG 0219SC 3A.)

59. Ibid., p.4.

60. Ibid., p.6.

61. Homework: LA response to DES. *Library Association Record* 87(9), September 1985, p.333.

62. Ibid.

63. Ibid.

64. Great Britain, Department of Education and Science. *Curriculum 11-16: towards a statement of entitlement.* HMSO, 1983, p.30.

65. *The school library resource service and the curriculum 'before five' to 'sixteen plus'.* Motherwell: Scottish Library Association, 1985, p.5.

66. *Recommended salary grades and conditions of service for school librarians 1984/85.* Library Association, 1984, p.1. (Salary Guide No.9.)

67. Great Britain, Office of Arts and Libraries. *School libraries: the*

foundations of the curriculum. Report of the Library and Information Services Council's Working Party on school library services. HMSO, 1984. (Library Information Series No.13.)

68. Ibid., p.11.

69. *Recommended salary grades and conditions of service for school librarians 1984/85.* Library Association, 1984, Paragraph 2.3. (Salary Guide No.9.)

70. *Library resource centres in secondary schools: guidelines and recommendations.* Nottinghamshire County Council, 1985, p.3.

71. MacDonald, M M, ed. *Towards excellence: case studies of good school libraries.* Library Association, 1984, p.60.

72. Thomson, L and Meek, M. *Developing resource-based learning: one school's approach.* Longman, 1985, p.69.

73. Ibid, p.84.

74. Library and Information Services Committee (Scotland). *Library services and resources for school education in Scotland. Report of a working party on current provision.* Edinburgh: National Library of Scotland, 1985, p.26.

75. MacDonald, M M, ed. *Towards excellence: case studies of good school libraries.* Library Association, 1984, p.50.

76. Ibid.

77. Great Britain, Department of Education and Science. *Report by HM Inspectors on a survey of secondary school libraries in six local education authorities. Carried out February-May 1984.* Department of Education and Science, 1985, p.19.

78. Thomson, L and Meek, M. *Developing resource-based learning: one school's approach.* Longman, 1985, p.78.

79. MacDonald, M M, ed. *Towards excellence: case studies of good school libraries.* Library Association, 1984, pp.41-42.

80. Ibid., p.45.

81. Ibid., p.59.

82. *Times Educational Supplement,* 1 February 1985.

83. Great Britain, Department of Education and Science. *Report by HM Inspectors on a survey of secondary school libraries in six local education authorities. Carried out February-May 1984.* Department of Education and Science, 1985, p.19.

84. *Library resource centres in secondary schools: guidelines and recommendations.* Nottinghamshire County Council, 1985, p.4.

85. Ibid.

86. MacDonald, M M, ed. *Towards excellence: case studies of good school libraries.* Library Association, 1984, p.54.

87. Great Britain, Department of Education and Science. *Aspects of secondary education in England: a survey by HM Inspectors of Schools.* HMSO, 1979.

88. MacDonald, M M, ed. *Towards excellence: case studies of good school libraries.* Library Association, 1984, p.41.

89. Ibid., pp.50-51.

90. Ibid., p.60.

91. Ibid., p.41.

92. Thomson, L and Meek, M. *Developing resource-based learning: one school's approach.* Longman, 1985, p.81.

93. MacDonald, M M, ed. *Towards excellence: case studies of good school libraries.* Library Association, 1984, pp. 47-48.

94. Ibid., p.48.

95. Klein, G. *The school library for multi-cultural awareness.* Trentham Books, 1985, p.43. (Education Libraries Bulletin, Special Supplement 23.)

96. Thomson, L and Meek, M. *Developing resource-based learning: one school's approach.* Longman, 1985, p.123.

97. *Report to the working party on school library services. The role*

and duties of the school librarian. Bedfordshire County Library, n.d. [Unpublished.]

98. Beswick, N W. Knowledge and skill requirements of the school librarian. Lecture given at a one-day workshop on *Educating school librarians*, organised by the School Libraries Group, and held at Loughborough University on 25 September 1985.

99. Ibid.

100. Pain, H. Survey of competencies required by school librarians: a report. *SLG News*, Autumn 1985, pp.11-13.

101. Pfister, F C. Competencies essential for school library media specialists. *Journal of Education for Librarianship* 23(1), Summer 1982, pp.29-42.

102. *Library resource provision in schools: guidelines and recommendations.* Library Association, 1977, p.15.

103. Great Britain, Office of Arts and Libraries. *School libraries: the foundations of the curriculum. Report of the Library and Information Services Council's Working Party on school library services.* HMSO, 1984, p.12. (Library Information Series No.13.)

104. Scottish Council for Educational Technology/Library and Information Services Committee (Scotland). Seminar on resources organisation in schools and educational resource services, 16 February 1984. Summary of working group reports appears in Appendix IV of Library and Information Services Committee (Scotland). *Library services and resources for school education in Scotland. Report of a working party on current provision.* Edinburgh: National Library of Scotland, 1985.

105. School Libraries Group of the Library Association. Letter to the Library Association, 9 May 1985.

106. *Educating school librarians*, organised by the School Libraries Group, and held at Loughborough University on 25 September 1985.

107. Beswick, N W. Knowledge and skill requirements of the school librarian. Lecture given at a one-day workshop on *Educating school librarians*, organised by the School Libraries Group, and held at Loughborough University on 25 September 1985.

108. Great Britain, Office of Arts and Libraries. *School libraries: the foundations of the curriculum. Report of the Library and Information Services Council's Working Party on school library services.* HMSO, 1984, p.13. (Library Information Series No.13.)

109. Library and Information Services Committee (Scotland). *Library services and resources for school education in Scotland. Report of a working party on current provision.* Edinburgh: National Library of Scotland, 1985, p.45.

110. Great Britain, Department of Education and Science. *Part-time advanced further education: an HMI survey of vocational courses.* HMSO, 1985.

111. Ray, S. Courses in school librarianship for teachers and librarians. Lecture given at a one-day workshop on *Educating school librarians*, organised by the School Libraries Group, and held at Loughborough University on 25 September 1985.

112. Scottish Council for Educational Technology/Library and Information Services Council (Scotland). Seminar on resources organisation in schools and educational resources services, 16 February 1984. Summary of working group reports appears in Appendix IV of Library and Information Services Committee (Scotland). *Library services and resources for school education in Scotland. Report of a working party on current provision.* Edinburgh: National Library of Scotland, 1985.

113. Great Britain, Office of Arts and Libraries. *School libraries: the foundations of the curriculum. Report of the Library and Information Services Council's Working Party on school library services.* HMSO, 1984. p.13. (Library Information Series No.13.)

114. *Recommended salary grades and conditions of service for school librarians 1984/85.* Library Association, 1984, Paragraph 2.4. (Salary Guide No.9.)

115. *Nalgo charter for non-teaching staffs in schools and colleges.* Nalgo, n.d., p.1.

116. Analysis of Library Association vacancy supplements 1981-1985, undertaken by Hilary Ghani, Department of Library and Information Studies, Loughborough University. [Unpublished.]

117. *Nalgo charter for non-teaching staffs in schools and colleges.* Nalgo, n.d., p.12.

118. *Recommended salary grades and conditions of service for school librarians 1984/85.* Library Association, 1984, Paragraph 3.2. (Salary Guide No.9.)

119. Ibid.

120. Ibid., Paragraph 3.4.

121. Ibid., Paragraph 2.5.

122. Great Britain, Office of Arts and Libraries. *School libraries: the foundations of the curriculum. Report of the Library and Information Services Council's Working Party on school library services.* HMSO, 1984. (Library Information Series No.13.)

APPENDIX 1

Staffing, stock and financial provision in secondary school libraries in England, 1979

Table 7: Maintained secondary school librarians — England, March 1979, by category of staff

	Type of school				
	1-16 Compre-hensive	11-18 Compre-hensive	Selective	Total[1]	
Number of schools	103	189	85	386	
Percentage of schools where the school librarian was a:					
Teacher librarian with no library qualifications	76	57	87	69	
Teacher librarian with Library Certificate	9	8	2	7	
Teacher librarian also professionally qualified librarian	2	3	2	3	
Professionally qualified librarian	7	21	2	13	
Other	6	11	4	8	
No response or no librarian	1	–	2	1	

1 Including nine sixth form colleges. The school librarians in these colleges were distributed as follows: six teacher librarians with no qualifications, two qualified librarians; one college did not complete the question.

Table 8: Maintained secondary school library books — England, March 1979. Books by type

	Type of school				Total
	11-16 Comprehensive	11-18 Comprehensive	Sixth form college	Selective	
Number of schools	103	189	9	85	386
Total library books (000s)	644.0	1817.0	81.5	505.9	3048.4
Percentage of stock classified as:					
Fiction	35	27	12	32	29
Non-fiction	56	68	83	61	64
Reference	8	5	5	7	6
Percentage of total stock on loan from the School Library Service	11	8	4	11	9

Table 9 : Maintained secondary schools — England, financial year 1978-79. Recurrent expenditure (£) per 100 pupils — category of expenditure

Recurrent expenditure (£) per 100 pupils	*Type of school*				Total
	11-16 Comprehensive	11-18 Comprehensive	Sixth form college	Selective	
Library books	83	100	134	81	93
Library periodicals	7	11	32	10	10
Library audio-visual material	5	4	14	6	5
Other library expenditure	8	8	14	9	8
Total	103	123	194	106	116

Source: Great Britain, Department of Education and Science. *Secondary school library survey.* HMSO, 1981. (Statistical Bulletin 7/81.) This material is reproduced with the permission of the Controller of Her Majesty's Stationery Office.

APPENDIX 2

Checklist of HMI recommendations, 1985

Taken from Report... on a survey of secondary school libraries in six local education authorities (HMSO, 1985) (provided by Jan Condon, Librarian, Solihull Sixth Form College. *SLG News* 12, Autumn 1985, pp.10-11). Reproduced by permission.

Accommodation:

1. Adequate in size for staff and pupils and its functions (2.2).
2. 1 seat per 15 pupils at least (2.3).
3. Not to be used as a classroom (2.2).
4. Available to pupils and staff without restriction (2.2).
5. Easy access to support and extend the work of individuals and departments (2.2).
6. Well and suitably furnished — importance of atmosphere (2.4).
7. Welcoming environment might include carpets, curtains, comfortable seats, suitable study furniture, displays of pupils' work, book exhibitions, plants, ceramics etc. (2.4).
8. Guidance should be bold, clearly visible from a distance (2.5).

Staffing:

9. A professional librarian is a considerable asset (3.1).
10. Time allowed to teacher-librarians important in order to be able to fulfil duties (3.2).
11. Constant adult presence necessary for development and use (3.3).
12. Assumption that the library is the province of the English Department is false — all Departments should be involved (3.5).
13. Involvement of pupils of value to pupils (3.7).
14. Librarian should be responsible to member of the senior management team (3.5).
15. Librarian should have access to body making curriculum decisions (head of department meetings etc.) (3.6).
16. Low status and pay scales noted and head of department status implied as desirable (3.6).
17. Access to INSET and other courses (3.9).
18. LEAs should review their provision of courses for teacher-librarians and professional librarians (3.9).

Stock:

19. Location a matter of school policy (4.1).
20. Advantages of having a coordinated organisation of resources and a comprehensive catalogue (4.1).
21. Central provision provides best access to resources (4.2).
22. Ten or more books per pupil a reasonable figure (4.3).
23. The stock should be appropriate in quantity, quality, range and match for the school (4.4).
24. School library services should be exploited for material and professional help and advice (4.6,4.7).
25. A good range of periodicals and newspapers should be provided (4.8).
26. The stock should be constantly reviewed and updated (4.9).

Finance:

27. Active life of a book on average may be 10 years; a school needs to budget for 10% replacement of stock each year. There is a direct connection between the finance made available to a library and its use (5.7).

Organisation:

28. There should be no unnecessary restrictions and prohibitions to inhibit use (6.1).
29. The library should be open as often as possible, preferably before and after school (6.2).
30. Use should be made of servicing of new books by suppliers (6.3).
31. Leaflets or handbooks for pupils and staff should be made available, describing layout, organisation and facilities (6.4).

Use:

32. Library should be an integral part of the life and work of a school (7.1).
33. Departments should be able to borrow collections for use in the classroom (7.1).
34. The support of the Headteacher is crucial (7.6).
35. Library skills courses should have aims and be purposeful and should take account of instruction and experience received in the primary school (7.7).
36. Library should be involved in study skills. The necessary training should be made available (7.8).

37. Information technology should be developed in libraries. Help and advice should be given (7.9).
38. Subject departments should be involved in the selection, review and maintenance of stock in relevant sections of the library (7.10).
39. School libraries benefit from the active involvement of the advisory service and especially from the school library service (7.11).

APPENDIX 3

School book spending: some facts

Fact 1

DES *Statistical Bulletin 10/84* provides a breakdown of local education authority spending in England for 1982/83. Books represent 0.8% of current spending; metropolitan districts spending on average less per pupil on books and equipment than the non-metropolitan and London authorities.

Fact 2

Sir Alan Bullock, in his foreword to *School libraries: the foundations of the curriculum* (HMSO, 1984, p.v), states that from the second quarter of 1983 to the same period in 1984 sales of books to United Kingdom primary and secondary schools fell by 12.85% in value:

> Even when allowance is made for the rise in prices, this is a disturbing figure. It strongly suggests that, when local education authorities and schools are under pressure to economise, many of them see school libraries an obvious area in which to make cuts — and to go on making them.

Fact 3

The following are updated figures, produced for spending on school books by the National Book League, which were originally produced in the report of its working policy on *Books for schools* (NBL,1979).

	Secondary school library books		
	1981/82	*1983/84*	*1984/85*
Recommended figures to LEAs for expenditure per pupil to ensure:			
a good standard of provision	£5.78	£6.77	£7.14
a reasonable standard of provision	£4.99	£5.85	£6.15

Compare these figures with HMI figures found in its *Report . . . on a survey of secondary school libraries in six local education authorities* (DES, 1985, p.12).

Expenditure per pupil	£0.0	2 schools
	0.01 - 0.50	14 schools
	0.51 - 1.00	13 schools
	1.01 - 1.50	12 schools
	1.51 - 2.00	11 schools
	2.01 - 2.50	1 school
	2.51 - 3.00	1 school
	over 3.01	5 schools

Also compare with figures produced by the Association of Librarians in Schools (ALIS), which surveyed library allowances in Nottinghamshire secondary schools.

	1982/83	*1983/84*
Average allowance per pupil	2.40	2.37
Minimum allowance per pupil	.53	1.25
Maximum allowance per pupil	4.55	4.16
Minimum amount	400	800
Maximum amount	7000	5000

APPENDIX 4

Staffing of UK secondary school libraries, 1984

(from the Educational Publishers Council's *Survey on expenditure in secondary school libraries*, published in 1985, pp.3-4). Reproduced by permission.

How is the library staffed? (excludes independent schools)

Teacher Librarian & 'Other'	28.3% (146)
Chartered Librarian only	23.6% (122)
Teacher Librarian only	20.0% (103)
Chartered Librarian & 'Other'	12.2% (63)
'Other' only	9.3% (48)
Chartered & Teacher Librarian	2.9% (15)
Chartered & Teacher Librarian &'Other'	2.3% (12)
No Staff	1.4% (7)

Independent schools library staffing

Teacher Librarian & 'Other'	35.0% (14)
Teacher Librarian only	30.0% (12)
Chartered Librarian only	15.0% (6)
Chartered & Teacher Librarian	7.5% (3)
Chartered Librarian & 'Other'	7.5% (3)
Chartered & Teacher Librarian & 'Other'	2.5% (1)
'Other' only	2.5% (1)
No Staff	– (–)

APPENDIX 5

The employment of professional school librarians in Scotland, 1985

Regional Education Authorities		
Central	21	
Fife	7	
Grampian	21	
Lothian	42	(also one who is part-time only)
Highland	16	
Strathclyde		
Argyll	1	
Ayr	21	
Dunbarton	8	
Glasgow	20	
Lanark	33	
Renfrew	25	
Dumfries and Galloway	2	
Orkney	2	
Shetland	1	
Western Isles	1	
Tayside		
Dundee	5	
Perth and Kinross	3	(term time only)

Overall total 230

Source: Library and Information Services Committee (Scotland). *Library services and resources for school education in Scotland. Report of a working party on current provision.* Edinburgh: National Library of Scotland, 1985. Appendix 1. Reproduced by permission.

APPENDIX 6

The employment of professional school librarians in English and Welsh counties, 1985

COUNTIES:

with fewer than 5	*with fewer than 10*	*with fewer than 20*	*with fewer than 30*	*with fewer than 40*
North Yorkshire	East Sussex	Avon	Derbyshire	Cheshire*
Norfolk	Lancashire	Surrey	Hertfordshire	Bedfordshire
Essex	Warwickshire*			Suffolk
Salop*	Kent*			
Somerset	West Sussex*			
Cumbria	Hampshire			
Isle of Wight*				
Cornwall				
Northamptonshire				
Wiltshire*				
Buckinghamshire				
Oxfordshire				
Cambridgeshire				
Northumberland				
Dorset				
Hereford & Worcestershire				

with fewer than 5 (contd.)	
Gwynedd*	*with 40+*
Dyfed*	Nottinghamshire (65)
Clwyd*	

* Includes/represents librarians seconded from the public library service.

The following authorities employ peripatetic school librarians, responsible for a number of schools:

Powys
Norfolk
Berkshire
Suffolk

Source: Data collected by David Fuegi, Library Adviser, Office of Arts and Libraries.

APPENDIX 7

After LISC[34]: England and Wales local authority plans and developments

Bexley : aiming to pursue the formation of a policy statement on the role of the library in the school.

: provision of full-time short course for school staff involved in libraries.

: a pilot scheme whereby a chartered librarian would be appointed with responsibility for a number of school libraries, concentrating on the care of bookstocks, allowing teachers to give their time to developing information skills.

Bolton : the Education and Arts Committee has resolved to ask headteachers and governors to consider the need to provide adequate professional and clerical staff time to allow the library to function efficiently.

Brent : the Education Committee has agreed to the principle of professional librarians being employed in all secondary schools.

Buckinghamshire : establishment of a phased programme for chartered librarians in schools.

Cambridgeshire : school library provision has been surveyed, and provided cause for concern. Guidelines to be produced upon which policies are to be based.

: recommending employment of professional librarians in schools, seconded from the library service.

Devon : the Policy Committee has agreed to £150,000 being set aside for funding library initiatives in Devon schools, intended to make significant improvements in the standard of school library provision in the county. The local education authority will match every £1 a school puts forward for the development of its library and resource provision with £3.

: the Schools Sub-committee has agreed to the appointment of an advisory teacher for libraries and resources.

Doncaster : the library service is continuing to press the case for better staffing of school libraries, preferably by the appointment of suitably qualified staff.

Dorset : the library service is recommending the employment of professional librarians in schools.

Durham : the library service is hoping to work closely with the Education Department to encourage the employment of chartered librarians in schools.

Gateshead : the local authority has agreed to the library service's recommendation that a chartered librarian should be appointed to each tertiary college on Scale 6.

: augmenting school library service to provide a service to secondary schools.

: hoping for long term attitudinal change leading to the employment of professional librarians in every secondary school.

Hampshire : Secondary School Challenge Scheme allocating to schools £9000 over three years (£3000 per year) for additional resources.

Hertford-shire : hope for additional posts for school librarians, the greatest difficulty being finance.

: £10,000 being redeployed from April 1986 to provide revitalisation of 10 school libraries.

: undertaking a detailed survey of provision and use.

: intending to provide case studies of good practice.

Kirklees	:	hoping to increase expenditure by schools on books by allocating £158,000 per year from Education and £78,750 from Leisure budgets.
	:	report approved which asks for consideration to be given to employing professionally qualified librarians seconded from the library service.
Leicester-shire	:	possibility of a pilot project which could establish the potential of employing professional librarians in schools.
Liverpool	:	the Council has agreed to all secondary schools having library ancillary staffing from September 1985, these having head of department status and graded Scale 3.
	:	consider dual qualification desirable.
North Tyneside	:	wishes to employ dual-qualified or professional librarians in high schools, but finance not yet forthcoming. Continuing to press for this.
North Yorkshire	:	surveying library provision and use.
	:	producing local guidelines.
Northum-berland	:	approved appointment of professional librarian to a dual-use high school library
	:	considering delegation of additional funding for ancillary staffing in school libraries.
Redbridge	:	recommending employment of peripatetic secondary school librarians.
Sheffield	:	intention to implement policy for professional librarians to be appointed to comprehensive schools, but problem of limited finance.
Solihull	:	survey of school libraries demonstrating cause for concern.
	:	the library service's major recommendations include professional librarians in schools with adequate clerical assistance.

Wakefield	:	working party of officers to consider the differences in school library provision.
West Sussex	:	the library service has established a working party with the Education Department.

Source: Data collected by David Fuegi, Library Adviser, Office of Arts and Libraries.

APPENDIX 8

Job description of senior school librarian, Nottinghamshire

a) Responsible to the Head Teacher for providing a service to teachers and guidance to pupils on the School Library.

Specifically responsible for the following duties and responsibilities:

1. Plan and oversee the organisation and workload of libraries/resource centres, including setting targets and objectives, and monitoring achievements, without direct professional supervision. Consultation with school Senior Management teams regarding the most effective patterns of use by pupils and staff, and the educational aims and philosophy of the school as reflected in the Library/Resource Centre, including the submission of written reports and proposals for development.

2. Contribute to the development of the curriculum through attendance at formal meetings of the academic management team, faculty and departmental discussions, and informal liaison with individual teachers. Advise on the availability, suitability and use of appropriate printed and other resources including viewdata, teletext and other information technology sources.

3. Selection and acquisition of all stock to meet the needs of the whole range of pupils and staff. Such provision should cover the full ability range and take account of the social and ethnic background of the school population. The subject fields and professional developmental needs of the teaching staff should also be reflected. Maintenance of the stock, including decisions on withdrawal and replacement of worn-out and out-of-date materials.

4. Financial management and administration of library budget for books, materials and stationery. Preparation of financial estimates, and an annual report to the Head Teacher on requirements for stock maintenance and development to satisfy future needs in the light of curriculum development, new courses, etc.

5. Arrangement of materials for effective retrieval, including systematic indexing, classification and cataloguing of all the school's resources.

6. Guidance and assistance to:

   (i) Pupils, on

      (a) appropriate strategies for the selection of information sources to undertake assignments both from within the school, and the wider community

      (b) the effective use of specific sources

      (c) the choice of literature to meet curricular and leisure needs

      (d) the compilation of booklists, where appropriate.

   (ii) Teachers, on

      (a) learning materials appropriate to the whole range of courses

      (b) professional reading

      (c) background information to various aspects of the curriculum.

7. Participation with the teaching staff in the school's development of language and information skills programmes; in particular those areas which involve the development of bibliographical and information retrieval skills.

8. Liaison with outside organisations:

   (a) ensure that appropriate materials are obtained from outside interlending agencies.

   (b) responsibility for personal professional development, making full use of advisory services, in-service training, and sharing knowledge and expertise with other colleagues.

   (c) keep abreast of current children's literature and developments in education and librarianship.

9. Direction and training of clerical assistant(s), where appropriate.

10. Ensure a high standard of appearance, display and promotional material for the library/resource centre, in order to provide an appropriate environment conducive to the optimum exploitation of library facilities.

Source: Library resource centres in secondary schools: guidelines and recommendations. Nottinghamshire County Council, 1985, p.17.

b)... it is crucial that the Librarian's role and place within the school be clearly defined. Most school librarians now are graduates with a post-graduate diploma or Master's degree in librarianship, sometimes with a PGCE. They have to have completed several years post-qualification *supervised* service before being eligible for election as an Associate of the Library Association and receiving the Library Association's Charter.

In terms of the capital value of the building, equipment and stock, the librarian controls an expensive asset within the school and it therefore makes good sense to ensure that he/she can fulfil the Librarian's role effectively, in terms of:

(i) provision; and

(ii) exploitation of books and learning resources.

So that he/she can readily evaluate the curricular, information and recreational needs of the school, the Librarian must have the opportunity to discuss, both formally and informally, with senior colleagues; involvement in curriculum planning and departmental meetings; and a direct link to the senior management of the school, e.g. through the Deputy Head (Curriculum). In short, the Librarian should be regarded as the equivalent of a Head of Department, whose awareness of literature and resources, of links in the information and book supply networks, of ways of indexing, storing and retrieval of information and of ways of finding out what is not immediately known, makes him/her a key figure for both staff and pupils, whose influence is not restricted to any one group or subject area.

The Librarian also has a role to play in the pastoral/social life of the school.

His/her major role, however, is in acting as a link, a facilitator, between the requirements of the curriculum and the materials available.

Most librarians are now involved with interdisciplinary teams in school in the development of study skills and user education programmes, and in the presentation of such programmes to pupils, both formally and in the course of their day-to-day work as readers' advisers.

Library promotion can be developed in many ways, e.g. provision of multimedia displays, production of reading lists, and the running of informal lunchtime and after-school sessions, which also allow for feedback from the children on their reading and outside interests.

The professional school Librarian is the manager of a centralised resource which supports, but also extends beyond, the needs of the curriculum, to develop the skills and awareness necessary for lifelong learning. He/she is a professional member of staff who provides an extra dimension of expertise within the school, which can be used by staff and pupils alike, whilst maintaining a balanced objectivity to benefit the school as a whole.

Source: Library resource centres in secondary schools: guidelines and recommendations. Nottinghamshire County Council, 1985, p.7. Reproduced by permission.

APPENDIX 9

Job description for school librarians in Newcastle upon Tyne

The three major responsibilities of school librarians are:

1. To purchase or otherwise acquire a range of materials relevant to the curriculum and suitable for the teaching and learning needs of staff and pupils at all levels of ability.

In order to support the curriculum in this way school librarians need to be familiar with its objectives and the subjects taught within it. This involves the following tasks:

i) frequent consultation with teaching staff and heads of subject departments

ii) attendance at Head of Department and curriculum planning meetings

iii) checking of catalogues and bibliographies to locate materials and keep informed about new publications

iv) visiting booksellers to purchase material

v) ensuring library budgets (£3,000 – £4,000 per school) are spent within the appropriate time span

vi) liaison with outside agencies such as Education Library Service, City Library, Teachers Centre and other potential sources of information or materials

vii) keeping a check on the balance of stock to ensure coverage of all subjects, ages and ability levels

viii) dissemination of information about library resources to staff and pupils.

2. To ensure that all pupils are able to use the school library confidently and effectively and to provide an environment in which pupils can learn and practise techniques of enquiry and research. To do this school librarians need to:

i) determine modes of organisation of the library

ii) classify, catalogue and index material

iii) prepare and carry out library induction programmes

iv) be involved in preparing and teaching study skills and information retrieval courses

v) reinforce what is learnt in these sessions by giving individual help and guidance to pupils in their search for appropriate material.

3. To foster and develop the reading habit and encourage reading for leisure as well as information. In order to achieve this school librarians must:

i) provide individual reading guidance

ii) be knowledgeable and informed about literature for children and young adults

iii) produce booklists, displays and exhibitions

iv) run school bookshops

v) be involved in promotional activities such as author visits, readings, storytelling and talks to parents.

In addition to the above, school librarians must also plan and prioritize the work of the library assistants and attend meetings arranged by the Education Librarian on three half-days each month.

Reproduced by permission.

APPENDIX 10

Job description of school librarian: Margaret Dane School, Hertfordshire

i) The librarian works in close cooperation with the Head of Resources and is answerable to the Head who retains overall responsibility for the academic development of the school. She is a member of the staff common room, the full-time staff meeting and the subject heads' meeting and may attend any other meeting open to members of the teaching staff, e.g. Staff Association, Curriculum Forum. She shares with the teaching staff the common responsibilities outlined in the staff handbook.

ii) The librarian has full responsibility for the routine running of the library. This includes:

submitting an annual budget, discretionary ordering, negotiating with County Equipment and Architects' Department

selecting, training and authorizing pupil librarians at all levels

choosing, buying and processing all library books

administering and maintaining the loan system

ensuring that the management and provision of the library supports the aims of the school as a whole

establishing an effective system of communication with all members of the school community

ensuring that the function of the library is clearly understood by pupils, staff and parents.

iii) The librarian is expected to liaise fully with the different departments of the County Library Service, local public and academic libraries, and professional bodies, for both the advantage of the school and her own professional development.

She has the same rights as any member of the teaching staff to seek approval for visits and training courses.

iv) Since the library is the heart of the curriculum, the librarian has a professional responsibility to participate fully in planning and implementing any aspects of the school curriculum which involve the library. This includes:

ensuring that appropriate library skills are taught in each year (this may require liaison with primary schools) and in each of the four main curricular areas, either directly or through subject syllabuses

contributing to induction courses, pastoral programmes and general studies, and specialist lessons where appropriate

assisting with materials and advice any staff member engaged in subject or educational research, any girls involved in independent learning programmes, groups engaged on projects, and staff groups planning the curriculum

promoting reading and the development of good reading habits by the arrangements of the library, by cooperation with the School Bookshop and Swopshop, and by exchange of information and ideas with staff, pupil librarians and sixth-formers

v) The librarian is expected, like other staff members, to make such provision that her work can carry on smoothly in her absence, and to monitor the effectiveness of her work in whatever ways seem appropriate.

Source: MacDonald, M M, ed. *Towards excellence: case studies of good school libraries.* Library Association, 1985, pp.67-69. Reproduced by permission.

APPENDIX 11

A list of ideas and practices which the 'most successful school libraries' have adopted in order to fulfil their functions

i) The role of the library within the school, as a support to the curriculum, has been clearly understood by the Head Teacher, other staff and pupils.

ii) Their view of the nature of learning and the scope of the curriculum, and their statement of curriculum aims, includes an appreciation of the services the school library can offer, and of the *skills,* e.g. information retrieval, handling of learning resources, and study skills, which must be taught to enable pupils to make use of the library.

iii) All sources of information, whether printed, audio-visual or electronic, are integrated in the library-resource centre, with a complete index to all resources.

iv) Departments have been persuaded of the inter-disciplinary uses of many information sources, and of the value of 'pooling' resources for the whole school.

v) The Librarian is regarded as a key figure in the learning process, and therefore in the school hierarchy.

vi) The stock is adequate in quantity, relevant in content and attractive in condition, and finance is provided at a realistic level to maintain it.

vii) The library space is sufficiently large, well-planned, adequately furnished and equipped, to enable it to play its part as a central, rather than peripheral, part of the learning experience offered by the school.

Source: Library resource centres in secondary schools: guidelines and recommendations. Nottinghamshire County Council, 1985, p.4. Reproduced by permission.

APPENDIX 12

A list of professional roles and tasks recommended by the School Library Association if the school library is to be effective

1) *Promotion* — using all means to make the whole staff aware of the contribution that library resources can make to subject teaching and to education in the wider sense; being responsive to needs expressed by staff; encouraging all staff to use resources both in their teaching area and by bringing their classes into the library resource centre.

2) Determining modes of *organisation* — necessary paperwork, routines, housing and location of books and other media.

3) *Classifying* and *cataloguing* the materials; making classification decisions.

4) Keeping informed about *new publications* including children's and adolescents' fiction.

5) Organising *selection* of new stock; assisting the rest of the staff to make selection decisions (e.g. through lists, inspection copies, displays); selecting materials not thus covered, e.g. fiction, general reference, periodicals.

6) Keeping a check on the *balance of stock* to ensure coverage of all subject fields.

7) *Making available* books and materials for classroom use; providing lists of topic materials as needed.

8) Knowing of, and coordinating with, *outside agencies*, e.g. schools library service, museum service, teachers' centres, public libraries; promoting use of these by students and staff; arranging visits to school by outside experts.

9) *Liaison with audio-visual/reprographics department* regarding development of non-book stock and materials produced within the school.

10) Arranging *displays* in the library and elsewhere, including publicity for the library; liaison with subject departments for this purpose.

11) *Control and discipline* in the library; supervising at 'opening times'; ensuring access at all times of day; being personally present so far as time allows, and organising coverage for other times.

12) Participating as a member of the *curriculum and resources* committee; discussing implications for resources of all curricular proposals and suggesting ways of using and developing resources for curricular purposes; estimating and costing future needs and presenting the case.

13) Liaison with *primary-school* librarians, especially to ease pupils' transition to the secondary school.

14) Organising and participating in programmes of *library instruction/induction*, e.g. in 'library periods', including work related to specific subjects.

15) Encouraging *positive attitudes* to, and facility with, books and other media; promoting literacy and learning through effective use of the library by all students.

16) Regularly *helping individuals and groups* to locate and use resources; promoting self-reliance and self-confidence.

17) Promoting *involvement of pupils and parents* in the work of the library, as a social and educational benefit, and encouraging parents to be aware of the value of reading.

18) Ensuring that *accounts* are kept as necessary.

19) Supervising *ancillary staff* and instructing them in their duties.

Source: The way ahead : the organisation and staffing of libraries and learning resources in schools in the 1980s. School Library Association, 1980, pp.12-13. Reproduced by permission.

APPENDIX 13

Skills which should be developed if the DES educational aims are to be achieved

Communication

the ability to listen, speak, read and write effectively

the ability to use and interpret non-verbal and graphical means of communication

Observation

to observe accurately using all the senses and a variety of instruments, such as hand lenses and measuring devices

to observe details, similarities and differences

to observe sequences

Study

to discriminate and to classify

to recognise relationships (patterns) in data

to select and extract information from a variety of sources

to weigh and interpret evidence and to draw conclusions

Problem-solving

to ask pertinent questions

to propose alternative hypotheses and to help to design ways of testing them

to carry out fair tests

to apply knowledge and concepts to the solution of real-life problems

to predict on the basis of experience and data

to make informed choices

Physical and practical

to coordinate bodily movement and finer manual skills

to develop craft skills — cutting, shaping, joining

to select appropriate tools and items of equipment and to use them effectively

to write legibly
to use keyboards

Creative and imaginative

to envisage life at other times, avoiding anachronism, and in other places; to imagine life as it may appear to other people
to express ideas
to devise and design in various media including sound and movement

Numerical

to estimate and to measure
to understand and to formulate accurately relationships expressed in the four operations of arithmetic
to use numerical and spatial relationships and elementary graphical and statistical data

Personal and social

to meet personal needs such as dressing oneself, handling a knife and fork, using a telephone
to adjust to different social contexts
to consider others' views
to contribute, cooperate and take the lead as appropriate within groups
to accept responsibility.

Source: Great Britain, Department of Education and Science. *The curriculum from 5 to 16.* HMSO, 1985, pp.39-40. This material is reproduced with the permission of the Controller of Her Majesty's Stationery Office.

APPENDIX 14

Resourcing CPVE programmes

One of the underlying assumptions of all CPVE programmes is that the student needs to learn how to learn rather than needing to learn a specific set of facts within a particular subject discipline(1). CPVE courses are based almost entirely on the investigation, research, gathering, collating and presenting of information on areas which are as diverse as the students' own interests and abilities and which no teacher is naturally equipped to deal with fully(2).

Access to information

In this context the provision of an adequately resourced (3,4) library is vital. It is only through the centralised provision of information that all CPVE students within an institution can be guaranteed access as and when required to the fullest possible range of information sources. Given the unpredictability of individual students' choices of study, changing significantly from week to week or even day to day, no single subject department can hope to satisfy the information demands of these students.

Range of information sources

The types of information resource that are essential in the library include a wider than average collection of reference material(5), periodicals and periodical indexes and abstracts, cuttings files for fringe, ephemeral and fugitive material, microfiche, on-line links to external databases such as Prestel and The Times Network for Schools, statistical data, video films, audio tapes, slides and computer software, in addition to the standard texts and balanced collections of background material normally provided. It will also be necessary to provide in the library the equipment necessary to make use of these resources, such as microcomputers, microfiche readers and video recorders.

Staffing

Such increased provision will have considerable implications for the staffing of the library. Without the *full-time* presence of at least one professionally qualified librarian or teacher-librarian, severe restrictions will be placed in the way of student-centred learning. The librarian's role is crucial (6), not only in ensuring that the materials and facilities required are available at all times and are effectively organised, but also to help students in the processes of identifying, locating and using them. Because of the close involvement of the librarian in developing library user education programmes to meet the requirements of CPVE, in developing students' information handling skills and in guiding their use of information technology, the librarian needs to be involved in pupil profiling. The librarian also needs to participate in all curriculum development discussions (7) and staff development programmes both within the institution and, where applicable, within consortia. Close links at consortium level between librarians of participating institutions are also essential to facilitate the exchange of experience and resources. Where there is no consortium opportunities must be available for the librarian to develop close links with the Regional Curriculum Base resource centre and with the local authority's education library support service (8). Loan collections of project books and other materials relevant to CPVE students' needs should be provided within an authority through its education library service, to supplement the resources available within institutions.

References:

1. CPVE Guide
2. 14-18 curriculum: integrating CPVE, YTS, TVEI?
3. LA school library resource centres guidelines
4. LA guidelines for professional service and resource provision for college libraries
5. LA Guide to reference collections
6. FEU Statement on staff development for support staff in FE
7. OAL School libraries : foundations of the curriculum
8. SLG Directory of school library support services in the UK.

Source: The School Libraries Group of the Library Association.

APPENDIX 15

Park Comprehensive School, Nottinghamshire: library aims and objectives

1. To provide within the school a centralized resource of materials and expertise which responds to the formal and informal curricular needs of pupils and staff.

2. To enable pupils to acquire information and study skills in order to facilitate direction of their individual information needs.

3. To create an awareness of the role libraries and information skills play within the sphere of lifelong learning.

4. To encourage the use of a relevant fiction stock in order to extend reading ability, awareness and enjoyment of literature.

5. To inculcate the skills relevant to the location, retrieval and processing of information within the framework of the first year's Integrated Studies curriculum.

6. To develop the Lower School resource centre's integral role in the development of study and information skills.

7. To reinforce library and study skills throughout the curriculum in cooperation with the teaching staff in order to facilitate learning from the second year through to the needs of the fifth year external examinations.

8. To select, acquire and maintain book and other materials for the maintenance of a balanced current stock which reflects the needs of the formal and informal curriculum as well as the ability and age range of the pupils.

9. To provide a stimulating fiction stock which reflects ability and age range, encourages reading, extends awareness and promotes the enjoyment of literature.

10. To maintain a current awareness of books and other information sources in order that a balanced stock is maintained.

11. To create a working atmosphere within which the pupils feel in control of directing their information needs according to individual ability and needs.

12. To stimulate interest and provide information through the medium of display.

13. To promote awareness of the personal enjoyment of books and literature through extension and other activities centred on the Resource Centre and Library.

Source: MacDonald, M M, ed. *Towards excellence : case studies of good school libraries.* Library Association, 1985, p.57. Reproduced by permission.

APPENDIX 16

The kinds of activities that are undertaken by school librarians on a day-to-day basis

(a) *8.30 to approximately 9.00 a.m.* School library is open for borrowing and the school librarian may be very busy helping users to find the books and information they require, and issuing and discharging books.

(b) *Lessons start to lunch time.* Some of the time will be taken up with conducting library classes. These are periods where younger children, or those shortly to go on to higher studies, are trained in the use of the library. They are shown what is in the library, how it is arranged and how information can be found. In addition there may be groups brought in to be introduced to the resources of the library on a particular topic prior to undertaking specific project work.

Between these periods children and teachers may arrive singly or in small groups to find specific items of information needed for lesson preparation or topic work, or to study in the library. The librarian will not only be helping users to find the information required but will also be searching for books and materials, for use in the classroom or at home, which have been requested.

(c) *Lunch time.* The most hectic period in school libraries. It is not uncommon for up to 100 pupils to be in the library at this time, often with a librarian the only adult present. Willing pupils are frequently used as library helpers and deal with the issue desk so that the librarian can be free to maintain order and help children in the library to select appropriate materials. The maximum lunch break school librarians get is 30 minutes during which period the library is usually closed unless teachers have arranged cover for this period.

(d) *Afternoons.* Once again much of the time can be taken up with library classes and individual assistance to pupils and teachers. In between times during both mornings and afternoons the librarian will be undertaking any of the following tasks:

i) examining bibliographical and publishers' catalogues and marking up items likely to be of interest to teachers before circulating them to staff

ii) scanning newspapers and journals, cutting out relevant illustrations and articles, mounting, indexing and filing them. This is particularly valuable for popular modern topics such as terrorism on which there is insufficient up-to-date material

iii) discussing proposed curriculum and courses with staff to ensure that the stock reflects the courses run and that index entries can constantly be added reflecting the terminology used in school

iv) cataloguing and indexing of audio-visual material some of which may be located in the library. Other items may be held by departments but will be more widely used by virtue of being indexed in the central catalogue

v) using bibliographical tools for searching for specialised articles and items of information required by sixth formers or teachers. Often items located will then be obtained from the County Library, other public libraries or the National Lending Library at Boston Spa

vi) preparing lists which may draw attention to material available on a particular topic or be a means of encouraging children to read more widely by introducing particular titles to them

vii) preparation and setting up of displays either in the library or at suitable locations within the school. These act as a reminder of what the library has to offer and how it can respond to current interests or popular demands

viii) receiving requests from teachers for new acquisitions and adding to these orders from the library

ix) typing invoices for book orders (in some schools this is done by clerical staff in post)

x) unpacking and checking new books as they arrive, cataloguing, classifying and indexing them so that staff and pupils searching for information can locate appropriate items easily, filing cards in the catalogue

xi) preparing books for the shelves: accessioning, attaching label, plastic jacket, spine label with class number on it. Typing book card and book pocket (some of these jobs are done by pupil helpers, particularly after school)

xii) writing reminders and overdues for books not returned.

(e) *After school.* School libraries are always open after school to allow free access to pupils, some of whom may wish to borrow books for home reading, others of whom will be doing homework. School librarians are aware of the fact that the school library is the *only* library available to many children and actively encourage recreational use of the library (though after-school use can be conditioned by bussing arrangements). The after-school period is also used for catching up on daily chores, such as sorting the issues, shelving, filing catalogue cards etc. In many schools a number of pupil helpers may remain behind to assist in these tasks. The school librarian remains on the premises until after 4.30.

(f) *Occasional duties*

1) *Visits to School Library Centre.* The weekly visit to the School Library Centre and public library is a vital part of a school librarian's work although it can mean that the school library is closed for that afternoon if no cover can be provided. During these visits the school librarians search the shelves and collect together books on requested topics which they pack up and deliver to the teachers. Each centre has on display the children's and adults' books published that week which school librarians examine for suitable material to order for the school library and to bring to the attention of teachers. Materials suitable for the staff library will also be selected from the education collections on these visits. School librarians will also visit the nearest large branch for local history material, to collect more advanced books requested by staff and pupils and to search for requested information that they have been unable to locate in the school library or School Library Centre. Any material they are still unable to locate they will use the bib-

liographical sources at the branch to trace and borrow from libraries outside the county.

2) *Holiday periods*. Holiday periods are the only time available to school librarians in which to undertake tasks that need to be done without interruptions. This, therefore, is the time at which they will be :

a) stocktaking
b) evaluating and weeding stock and identifying any gaps in coverage that need to be rectified
c) preparing induction courses
d) preparing a guide to the library for pupils and teachers
e) preparing an annual report on the library's development during a year
f) catching up on the backlog of cataloguing, classification and indexing
g) cataloguing and indexing departmental materials, usually audio-visual
h) taking part in in-service training courses which are vital because of the school librarian's professional isolation
i) visiting the university bookshops etc. to ensure there is no relevant material available of which they are not aware
j) writing to publishers and other organisations for catalogues and other materials (such as wall charts) likely to be of value to the school.

Source: Bedfordshire County Library. Included in a *Report to the working party on school library services. The role and duties of the school librarian.* Unpublished, 1978. Reproduced by permission.

APPENDIX 17

The librarian's diary: one week in the working life of a school librarian

Monday

8.45 a.m.	'Think ahead' weekly staff meeting.
P 1 & 2	Put up displays in library — 'Third World' and 'World Religions'.
P 3	Visited Home Economics Dept. to see how reorganization of departmental resources is progressing. Discussed with teacher possible methods of indexing and suggested finding pupils who have worked for me as librarians, to continue sorting and filing materials.
P 4	Fourth-year English groups. Choosing books for topics for CSE 'orals'.
P 5	Third-year Biology group — work on pollution.
Lunch-hour	Visit by rep. from Schools Council to discuss use of the library in the lunch hour and the need for a 'quiet room'.
P 6	Phoned County Supplies about non-arrival of stationery order. First trial run of BL SIR programme on computer with sixth-form librarian and Head of Computer Studies.
P 7	English teacher from Newport Grammar School, Essex phoned; asked if he could use my library skills materials to illustrate a talk he is giving to English teachers in Essex. Wrote to MR at ASLIB. Answered two letters from schools wanting information on our learning skills programme. Photocopied reports for Head.

P 8	Third-year English library period — teacher not present, pupils exchanging books — to and from Resources Room — staff having problems with photocopier which kept jamming.
4 - 5.30 p.m.	Staff meeting.

Tuesday

P 1	First-year English period — teacher not present.
P 2	Third-year Classical Studies group — Ancient Greece. First-year English library period — teacher present, 'story-starters', slidesets, etc.
P 3	Discussed planning and organization of this year's third-year RE project with Head of RE. Project starts. As last year, I shall join meeting in hall each week for all pupils and teachers taking part, to discuss problems, stage pupils should have reached, new materials, etc. This year pupils will work together in groups, according to the topics they have chosen, and also visit the library in the same groups. Mr M will be in the library with me so that we can both help, question and advise.
P 4 & 5	Visit by librarian from school in Harrow, working on dissertation for MA — 'The role of the librarian in relation to study/information skills'.

Lunch with Head of Progress and Head of RE. Afterwards visitor worked in my office during lunch hour.

P 6	Fourth-year English groups — topics for CSE talks and choosing books.
P 7	Third-year English library period — teacher present — pupils choosing fiction — teacher helping.
P 8	Third-year English library period — teacher not present — also choosing materials for other projects — History, Classical Studies, etc.
4.30 - 6 p.m.	Meeting at Hatfield Advisory Unit for Computer

	Based Education, Working Party on 'Use of microcomputers in school libraries'.
Wednesday	
P 1 & 2	Fifth-year General Studies group — projects on 'Famous Scientists'. I talked about sources of information and materials available. Use of encycs., biog. dictionaries, etc., magazines.
P 3	Set up radio and cassette recorder to record BBC broadcast for Radiovision.
	First-year library period. Teacher present. 'Story starters', slidesets, materials for projects, etc.
P 4	Second-year English library period. Teacher not present. I gave back library skills booklets, which I had marked, and discussed results and problem areas, etc.
	Third-year Classical Studies group. Ancient Greece.
P 5	Second-year English library period — teacher present. Returned library skills booklets. Visit by Clerk of Works to check on problems still remaining due to building of library extension.
Lunch hour	Publisher's rep. arrived. Took him over to Staff Workroom to set up display.
P 6 & 7	Phone call from Adeyfield School, Hemel Hempstead — teacher and librarian would like to visit us to look at equipment, library shelving, etc. They have visited us before to talk about the role of the librarian in the curriculum.
	Computer time. Trial run of SIR programme.
P 8	Form period. Pupils from various classes to change books. Checked newspaper a/c.
Thursday	
P 1	Rang Boys' High School to arrange Primary/Secondary Liaison meeting for representatives from Margaret Dane, Boys' High and

	the Firs JMI. Primary school pupils will visit Science Depts. in the secondary schools, later this term.
	Rang school in Welwyn Garden City to see if they use Prestel to copy educational computer programmes via Telesoftware Project.
	Archives material wanted by Head.
P 2	First-year Science class — with teacher — working on 'Library Skills through Science' worksheets. Unit on 'Water'.
P 3	Discussed third-year Classical Studies project work with teacher. Arranged times when they can visit library for research. I will talk to them about sources of information, resources available, etc. Also discussed possible sixth-form visits to Hatfield Poly Library and Cambridge City Library.
P 4	Second-year English library period — teacher present. Returned library skills booklets to pupils.
P 5	Visited History Dept. to see how work is progressing in organization of their resources. Talked with Head of History about possible methods of indexing materials. She would like first-year to work in library period 2 tomorrow on history topics, Joan of Arc, etc.
Lunch hour	Library very crowded — 63 girls reading or working — others choosing books.
P 6	Third-year Careers group — from General Studies class. I talked about sources of information — books, reference books, magazines, newspapers, etc.
P 7	Visit from new school governor — tour of library — talked to him about the library and the curriculum — plans for use of computer, etc.
P 8	First-year Science pupils — with teacher — working on Science worksheets — unit on 'Insects'.

Friday

P 1	Talked to third-year Classical Studies group —

	sources of info., etc. All had specific topics on Ancient Rome — costume, houses, education, etc. Teacher was there to help. Both working together.
P 2	First-year History group. Teacher present. Topic — Joan of Arc. Very structured research. Pupils had been told to start with encyclopedias and then progress to other books for more detailed information.
P 3	In-service training visit from probationary teachers. Showed them resources. Talked about library skills courses and the library and the curriculum. Partnership between teacher and librarian. Philosophy behind development of learning skills programme.
P 4	Second-year library period. English lesson — teacher present. Returned library skills booklets and discussed with pupils.
P 5	Third-year English library period — teacher present. 'Story starters' slidesets, etc. Changing books, reading magazines.
Lunch hour	Computer Fund-Raising Committee meeting.
P 6	Phone call from Publishing Manager, Children's Book Dept., Longmans — rearranging visit to us to discuss study skills and the library and the curriculum. Worked on book orders and short loan requests.
P 7 & 8	Third-year RE project. Attended meeting in hall at start of first session. All pupils and teachers taking part. Mr M explained organization to pupils. Explained how the marks for the project will be divided and the percentage which will be given for original ideas and for quoting sources. Talked about note-taking. Groups (a) World religions — 37 pupils (b) Famous religious people — 34 pupils (c) Who was Jesus? — 12 pupils (d) Christian denominations — 3 pupils (e) Science and religion — 3 pupils

(f) Religion and the arts — 1 pupil

(g) Others — 6 pupils

Period 7 Group a plus c and d, visiting library

8 Group b plus e and f, visiting library

Mr M in library. Both of us helping pupils.

Source: Thomson, L and Meek, M. *Developing resource-based learning: one school's approach.* Longman, 1985, pp.70-73. Reproduced by permission.

APPENDIX 18

Research-orientated work at Park Comprehensive, Nottingham

Examples of work:

Research in design — Woodwork
Play needs of children — Childcare
Family violence — Religious Education
History of instruments — Music
Pictorial research — Art
Evidence research — History
World War II background — English
Punishment — Discussion Group
Duke of Edinburgh Award — Physical Education

The history course is 'heavily based upon skills and research-based approaches to learning . . . these being taught in a more balanced manner when library facilities exist and provide a broad range of books resources' (W Wilson, Head of History). In religious education the 'wide range of resources enables a flexibility in teaching approaches to be employed by the department' (Miss T Gill, Head of RE). The geography department use the libraries to 'enable pupils to research in-depth background details to supplement classroom teaching' (Mrs S Sharkey, Deputy Head of Geography). Within the Lower School science teachers are looking to the Resource Centre to 'extend science beyond the laboratory and to broaden learning skills in relation to science' (Mr M Stewart, Science Department).

From these statements it can be seen that the Library/Resource Centre has an effective cross-curricular role within the traditionally academic subjects but information and research skills are also necessary to the arts. Here the library plays 'an important part in providing information on processes, construction and history' but also provides 'pictorial and literary sources on which to base imaginative work' (Mr M Spicer, Head of Art). The CDT department use the libraries for 'research in order to encourage individual approaches to design and technology'.

Source: Marshall, M M, ed. *Towards excellence: case studies of good school libraries*, Library Association, 1985, pp.63-64. Reproduced by permission.

APPENDIX 19

Databases created by school librarians in Bedfordshire

Microquery	—	the Census database : used by a school librarian in collaboration with the Humanities Department to collect and manipulate data on the local population going back to the previous century. Microquery has also been used by two librarians to develop a fiction database.
Quest	—	a fast version of Microquery which is being used to compile an energy database for comparison with SIR, and to provide quick access to a sound and video recordings file.
SIR	—	an energy database with 50 keywords is being compiled, mainly for use by sixth formers.
CLAIRE	—	a large database of local sites schools can visit, experts, useful organisations and locally produced materials, based on the Microquery programme.
EDFAX	—	a BBC programme that simulates CEEFAX and which is being used to provide a school magazine, information about the library, ideas of books to read.
Prestel	—	the 380Z Prestel package allows the microcomputer to interact with Prestel, to store pages for use later, and also provides a Local Viewdata package which allows local pages to be developed, emulating Prestel in a manner similar to EDFAX. Two librarians with BBC machines are about to run a trial of Micronet 800 which allows the BBC to interact with Prestel in a similar manner. Most of the useful information so far seems to be at sixth form level, e.g. for economics students.

Source: Virginia Berkeley, Assistant County Librarian (Young People), Bedfordshire.

APPENDIX 20

Areas of knowledge and understanding essential to the good school librarian's work

1. Curriculum studies, learning theory and teaching methodologies, with special reference to pupil-active learning modes, information and study skills, language skills, reading across the curriculum, media skills, visual, aural and computer literacy.
2. The library in the personal development of the child, including imaginative and pleasurable reading, the information needs of children, and the encouragement of the pleasure of reading and enquiry.
3. Selection tools and library materials in all areas of the school library's concern, including imaginative materials, specialist subjects, and resources in both categories produced in-house; selection criteria, including multicultural and multifaith questions, and problems of sexism and racism.
4. Reference and enquiry work with children and teachers, including search strategies, use of print and non-print sources, on-line sources, information agencies, and reader-guidance.
5. The organisation of knowledge, including content analysis, classification, cataloguing, subject indexing, and computerised retrieval methods.
6. Library organisation and management, including the library's place in the school management structure, co-operation with other departments and with outside agents, and library promotion.

Source: Office of Arts and Libraries. *School libraries: the foundations of the curriculum. Report of the Library and Information Services Council's Working Party on school library services.* HMSO, 1984, pp.12-13. (Library Information Series No. 13.) This material is reproduced with the permission of the Controller of Her Majesty's Stationery Office.

APPENDIX 21

Essential and desirable competencies of a school librarian

Scorings for each competency

KNOWLEDGE	Essential	Desirable	Not req'd
general	35	7	
librarianship principles	32	11	1
school librarianship principles	36	7	
school librarianship trends	37	6	
information searching	39	4	
information sources	40	3	
information skills	40	3	
indexing	31	11	
bibliography compilation	25	15	1
materials selection	42	1	
display techniques	36	6	
technology and librarianship	29	14	
information technology	24	14	
computer use	28	15	
audio-visual equipment use	21	19	2
management principles	21	19	3
organisational management	33	9	1
financial management	33	9	1
time management	29	12	2
staff management	21	12	7
aims of education	31	12	
issues in education	23	19	
trends of education	24	18	
educational system	24	15	1
school organisation	37	5	1
curriculum development	33	8	
teaching methods	23	18	2
teaching information skills	43		
teaching study skills	39	3	1
learning methods	20	16	2
reading	30	11	1
pupil supervision	36	7	
child/teenage behaviour	25	17	1
child/teenage culture	22	18	2

SKILLS	Essential	Desirable	Not req'd
materials selection	41		2
materials processing	33	7	3
repair of materials	26	12	5
production of materials	21	18	4
stock revision	38	2	
information indexing	37	6	
information organisation	40	2	
information searching	39	3	
information	41	1	
library promotion	41	2	
the promotion of reading	37	5	
giving talks	34	7	1
display techniques	35	7	
teaching information skills	39	4	
pupil motivation	27	14	1
materials acquisition	40	3	
adult fiction	27	14	2
adult non-fiction	30	11	1
children's fiction	42	1	
children's non-fiction	41	2	
teenage fiction	42	1	
teenage non-fiction	42	1	
audio-visual materials	23	15	1
administrative procedures	31	11	1
library equipment	26	17	
library promotion	41	2	
promotion of reading	37	5	
giving talks	30	12	
pupil supervision	36	7	
planning	29	14	
financial management	33	8	1
staff management	27	8	8
communication	39	4	
report writing	31	11	1
meeting	33	10	
negotiating	35	6	1
evaluation	31	9	2
manipulation	26	10	5
diplomacy	35	17	

ATTITUDES

professional	40	2	1	confidence	38	5	
maturity	34	5	3	consistence	31	10	1
integrity	38	3		independence	34	9	
responsibility	42	1		perseverance	37	5	
objectivity	33	8		willingness to learn*	10	1	
practicality	37	6		empathy	31	11	
imagination	31	12		tolerance	39	3	
innovation	31	12		patience	41	2	
prudence	26	15	1	compassion	28	12	2
initiative	39	4		care	31	10	1
awareness	35	2		approachability	43		
dynamism	27	14	2	sociability	30	12	
enthusiasm	42			humour	39	4	
self-motivation	41	2		co-operation	38	1	
commitment	42	1		willingness to help	43		
conscientiousness	40	2		flexibility	41	2	
tenacity	35	8		diplomacy	38	5	
positivity	34	8					

*printed as "willingness to lean", so only those returned questionnaires where lean was altered to learn were taken into account.

Source: Pain, H. Survey of competencies required by school librarians: a report. *SLG News*, Autumn 1985, pp.11-13.

APPENDIX 22

Essential elements for inclusion in advanced courses of study for practising school librarians

— curriculum for primary, secondary and special educational needs in Scotland

— managing the school library resource centre, and the management of the information skills programmes and services

— school administration — staffing, educational administration, time-tabling

— curriculum development — the school library's role

— criteria for selection and evaluation of learning resources

— evaluation of the effectiveness of the resources and services in school library resource centres

— regional library services — management, financial aspects, advisory services, etc.

— design and planning of a library resource centre

— information technology and its implications for resource provision

— design and production of learning resources. Ways in which librarians can contribute.

Source: Library and Information Services Committee (Scotland). *Library services and resources for school education in Scotland. Report of a working party on current provision.* Edinburgh: National Library of Scotland, 1985, p.45. Reproduced by permission.

APPENDIX 23

School librarianship and the library schools: a survey

14 responses were received from 18 questionnaires distributed in 1985.

a) *Undergraduate courses*

1. *Is school librarianship integrated into the common core curriculum?*

Institution	*Name of core subject*	*Year taught*	*Time allocated*
Aberdeen, RGIT	Management	2	18 hrs.
Aberystwyth, CLW	Management	3	2 hrs.
Belfast, Queen's University	Library in Society	1	2 hrs.[1]
Brighton Polytechnic	Library and Community	2	18 hrs.[2]
City University	not applicable		
Dublin, University College	not applicable		
Liverpool Polytechnic	Development and Reading of Children and Young Adults	1	30 hrs.[3]
	Function and Management of Libraries	1	not possible to calculate
	Development and Reading of Children and Young Adults	2	30 hrs.[3]
	Function and Management of Libraries	3	not possible to calculate

Loughborough Technical College	Library Organisation	1	6/7 hrs.
	Library Organisation	2	6/7 hrs.
Loughborough University	Structures and Functions	2	1 hr.
	Automated Information Processing[4]	2	not possible to calculate
Manchester Polytechnic	User Communities	1	10 hrs. + seminars
Newcastle upon Tyne Polytechnic	Introduction to Librarianship and Information Studies	1	½ hr.
Polytechnic of North London	Descriptive and Analytical Course on Services and Processes	3	4 hrs. plus case studies
University of Sheffield	not applicable		
University of Strathclyde	Management	2	10 hrs[1].

Notes:

1. component is general on all forms of library service to children.
2. emphasis is on current issues in education.
3. includes a strong education component.
4. not possible to calculate, as examples used throughout course include reference to schools.

2. *Is school librarianship offered as a specialist teaching area (option/ elective etc.)?*

Institution	*Y/N*	*Name of course*	*Year in which taught*	*Hours allocated*
Aberdeen, RGIT	no			
Aberystwyth, CLW	yes	Management of Learning Resources	2 or 3	c 30 – 40 hrs.

Belfast, Queen's University	yes	Library Services to Young People	3	40 hrs. (8 hrs. specifically on schools)
Brighton Polytechnic	no			
City University	not applicable			
Dublin, University College	not applicable			
Liverpool Polytechnic	no			
Loughborough Technical College	yes	Library Services to Children and Young People	2 of two-year Dip.HE	2/3 hrs. p.w. (school librarianship represents a third of the course)
Loughborough University	yes	School Librarianship	3	20 hrs.
Manchester Polytechnic	yes	Young People in the Community	3	30 hrs. (10 hrs. on schools)
Newcastle upon Tyne Polytechnic	yes	Library Materials in the Service of Education	1,2,3	3 hrs. p.w.
Polytechnic of North London	no			
University of Sheffield	not applicable			
University of Strathclyde	yes	Management of School and Children's Libraries	3	20 hrs.(c 10 hrs. on schools)

b) *Postgraduate courses*

1. *Is school librarianship integrated into the common core curriculum?*

Institution	*Y/N*	*Name of core subject*	*Time allocated*
Aberdeen, RGIT	yes	Management	6 hrs.
Aberystwyth, CLW	yes	Management	2 hrs. (services to schools)
Belfast, Queen's University	yes	Management of Libraries	2 hrs. (promotion of children's work generally)
Brighton Polytechnic	not applicable, although plan an MA course with option in school librarianship		
City University	no		
Dublin, University College	no		
Liverpool Polytechnic	yes	Management	not possible to calculate, frequent references made
Loughborough Technical College	not applicable		
Loughborough University	yes	Management	20 hrs. (optional tutorial group)
		Administrative Structures	5 hrs.
		Information Processing	not possible to calculate, frequent references to school libraries
Manchester Polytechnic	no		
Newcastle upon Tyne Polytechnic	no		
Polytechnic of North London	yes	Management	2 hrs.
University of Sheffield	yes	Academic Libraries	not known
University of Strathclyde	no		

2. *Is school librarianship offered as a specialist teaching area (option/ elective etc.)?*

Institution	*Y/N*	*Name of course*	*Hours allocated*
Aberdeen, RGIT	no		
Aberystwyth, CLW	yes	Management of Learning Resources	60 hrs.
Belfast, Queen's University	yes	Library Services to Young People	40 hrs. (8 hrs. specifically on schools)
Brighton Polytechnic	not applicable		
City University	no		
Dublin, University College	no		
Liverpool Polytechnic	yes	Education Libraries	102 hrs. (? hrs. schools)
Loughborough Technical College	not applicable		
Loughborough University	yes	School Librarianship	20 hrs.
		Role of the Library in Education	c 10 hrs.
Manchester Polytechnic	yes	Child Studies	c 4 hrs. on school libraries
Newcastle upon Tyne Polytechnic	yes	Student Selected Study	c 7½ hrs. of tutorials
Polytechnic of North London	yes	Primary and Secondary Education and Use of Learning Resources	24 hrs.
		School Library Resource Centres	24 hrs.
University of Sheffield	yes	Studies in Educational Librarianship	1-2 hrs. p.w.

University of Strathclyde	no		

c) *Are there other courses relevant to school librarianship?*

Institution	*Y/N*	*Course*
Aberdeen, RGIT	no	
Aberystwyth, CLW	yes	in conjunction with the University Faculty of Education: M.Ed. in Educational Technology, includes Management of Learning Resources M.Ed. in Curriculum Studies (School Librarianship). 50% School Librarianship, 50% Education. M.Lib. School Librarianship and Management of Learning Resources. M.Lib. Specialised Studies : Management of Learning Resources.
Belfast, Queen's University	no	
Brighton Polytechnic	no	
City University	no	
Dublin, University College	no	
Liverpool Polytechnic	no	*but* envisaging course on uses of micros in school libraries
Loughborough Technical College	no	
Loughborough University	yes	MA (School Librarianship) BA(Hons) Education and Library Studies, will end 1987
Manchester Polytechnic	no	
Newcastle upon Tyne Polytechnic	yes	Short courses in related areas
Polytechnic of North London	no	*but* possible to study for an MA degree with school library slant

University of Sheffield	no	
University of Strathclyde	yes	B.Ed. fourth year option course on school libraries

d) *Additional comments*

Aberdeen, RGIT	School librarianship permeates many areas of the curriculum, and many students select school librarianship for project work on cataloguing, audio-visual materials, etc.
Belfast, Queen's University	Part-time lecturer responsible for most of children-centred courses.
Brighton Polytechnic	The majority of students take part in a part-time 10-week placement, these including school libraries.
City University	School librarianship is not relevant to this institution's interests.
Dublin, University College	Hoping to undertake research in topics related to school librarianship.
Liverpool Polytechnic	Field work possible in school libraries.
Loughborough Technical College	Difficult to quantify the amount of school librarianship taught as it permeates the course, as it is seen as an important aspect of librarianship.
Loughborough University	Additional relevant option is Non-Book Media, and tentatively commencing short courses for practising school librarians, commencing with one-day events. Actively publishing and researching in school librarianship.
Newcastle upon Tyne Polytechnic	CNAA. BA(Hons),BA. Librarianship and Post-graduate Diploma in Library in Information Studies are being revised, the proposed starting date being September 1986, and there should be opportunities to follow schoool librarianship 'pathways' through a modular structure. This school sees school librarianship as an expanding need.
University of Sheffield	Visits to school libraries are undertaken, and there are visiting speakers on this subject. Currently considering the introduction of a full elective on school librarianship.
University of Strathclyde	May be placing more emphasis on in-service courses for school libraries in the future.

Source: Survey undertaken by H Pain, 1985.

APPENDIX 24

Salary scales and equivalent salaries, July 1985

3,006	a1		
3,180	a2		
3,309	1		
3,516	2		
3,795	3	Scale1	
4,008	4		
4,281	5		
4,533	6	(added point)	
4,733	7	(age 21 point)	Misc.1/2
5,058	8		
5,301	9		Misc.3
5,550	10		
5,706	11		Misc.4
5,883	12	Scale 2	
6,078	13		
6,234	14		
6,399	15	Scale 3	
6,576	16		
6,756	17		
6,900	18		
7,167	19	Scale 4	
7,437	20		
7,713	21		
7,920	22		
8,154	23	Scale 5	
8,424	24		
8,697	25		
8,979	26		
9,282	27	Scale 6	
9,591	28		
9,975	29		
10,308	30	SO 1	
10,638	31		
10,950	32		
11,280	33	SO 2	
11,604	34		

11,850	35
12,168	36
12,513	37
12,885	38
13,308	39
13,662	40
14,025	41
14,385	42
14,748	43
15,111	44
15,453	45
15,831	46
16,194	47
16,551	48
16,908	49

APPENDIX 25

Examples of salary scales for school librarians

Bedfordshire	Scale 5/6	£7920 — £9591
Derbyshire	Scale 4	£6900 — £7713
ILEA		
Schools of fewer than 1100 pupils		£8964 — £10,416
1101 — 1850 pupils		£10,416 — £12,231
more than 1850 pupils		£11,868 — £14,496 (all plus London weighting of £1495)
Newcastle upon Tyne	Scale 5	£7920 — £8897
Nottinghamshire		
11-18 yrs schools with more than one library (also if school has a Lower School with resource centre)	Scale 5	£7920 — £8897
11-18 yrs with one library 11-18 yrs schools and Upper Schools	Scale 4	£6900 — £7713

APPENDIX 26

ALIS comparison of school librarian salaries with teachers and school secretaries 1983/84

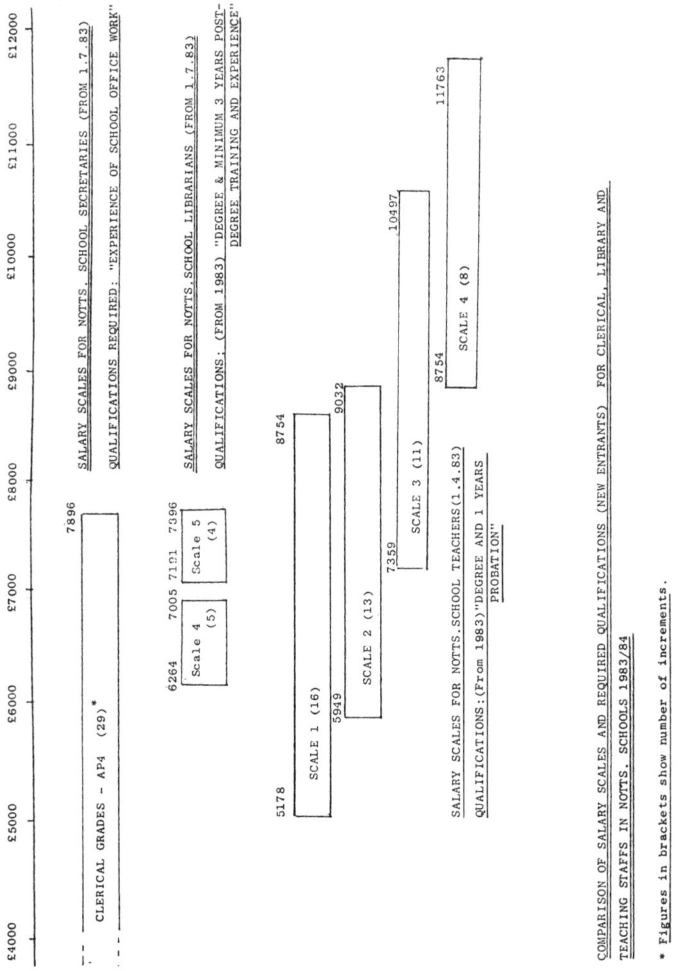

Other guides

British Library Information Guides are a new series of guides, directories and manuals in the field of librarianship and information science. Three other titles are listed below:

Family directory: information resources on the family edited by Jeffrey Weeks

BLIG 1. ISBN 0 7123 3075 5. 1986.

This directory provides a concise and accessible guide to information resources concerning the family, which will be readily used by researchers, practitioners, specialists and non-specialists alike. Its scope is wide, and though the main contents of this book concern the UK, it also contains a range of references to international resources.

Inventory of abstracting and indexing services produced in the UK by J Stephens

BLIG 2. ISBN 0 7123 3080 1. 1986.

This inventory updates LIR Report 21 of the same title, which is now out of print. The entries are arranged alphabetically by name of service. Four indexes are provided: broad subject headings, specific subject headings, an index of responsible authorities, and an index of database producers with the UK online databases they offer.

Archival collections of non-book materials: a listing and brief description of major national collections by Graham P Cornish

BLIG 3. ISBN 0 7123 3081 X. 1986.

The guide aims to give a description of the major national collections of non-book materials. Materials included in the survey are: sound recordings, visual recordings (film, video, photographs and slides), mixed media materials and graphics.